# Coffee &

# Kisses

Coffee & Kisses

# Coffee & Kisses

## MY JOURNEY BY

# Toni Barnett

Coffee & Kisses

**ISBN-13: 978-1540464934**

**ISBN-10: 1540464938**

# Acknowledgements

Thank you to my husband, Kevin, for encouraging me along this journey. Thank you to my children for the inspiration to grow and get better every day. Thank you Eric for all the hard work to finish this project and help me see another one of my dreams come true.

You are all amazing people, and I could not have done any of this without your love, your faith, and your devotion.

# Dedication

This book is dedicated to the four little Barnett children in my life. You all are truly my sunshine. Mama loves you all, back to the moon.

# Chapter **1**

**And so it began.**
**What does not break us, makes us stronger – but what**
**an experience.**
**Seek ye first the kingdom of God. To whom much is**
**given, much is required.**

## May 10th, 2014

At 8 pm, I left Brownwood, Texas in my Camry rental bound for San Angelo for workflow kick off on Monday. I was in the middle of a strange place, dressed in a business suit, wearing red high heels, and driving on a Sunday night surrounded only by the desolate sands, cacti, and cattle of Texas. On a whim, I glanced at the gas gauge. I soon realized three things: I had only a quarter tank of gas, I had no idea where a gas station was, and I had no cellphone service. Really, was there somewhere left in the United States that didn't have cell service? As my eyes told my mind it was almost dark, fear began to grip me.

I realized I would have to get gas, but I quickly concluded there were no signs for the next gas station. I grew up in a little town on the eastern side of Michigan where we usually had signs telling us how far until the next town or gas station. That was not the case in Texas. I had not become totally reliant on technology, so I didn't know that my GPS would tell me where the closest gas station was. I quickly learned to thumb through the GPS and find out what it had to offer. The nearest station was about an hour away. I was glad I hadn't learned to use my phone for GPS; otherwise, I would have been going nowhere fast.

I drove for about an hour and watched the gas gauge get lower and lower. During that time, I saw one trailer house parked about one quarter of a mile off the road. As a single white woman, a few things crossed my mind. If I ran out of gas, how long before someone would find me? Would I freak out if I had to park on the side of the road all night? How would it look if I walked back to that trailer in my red high heels and asked for help? Would they even let me on their property? Maybe I should have gotten my gun permit and gone to the shooting range.

I prayed a lot and asked The Lord not to let me run out gas. He answered my prayers and I finally saw the lights of the gas station. Back on the highway, I realized I needed to keep better records of all the experiences where I let God be in complete control. When I did that, I didn't get anxious. After a few hours, I was safely in my hotel room in San Angelo.

I immediately called my husband. "Kevin, how long would it take before you figured out that something had happened to me?" That got his attention.

"Toni, what are you talking about?" he asked over the din of our four children talking at once in the background.

The point of my question was not to make Kevin feel bad or look like a terrible husband. The goal was to make us realize we were not very attentive to our respective schedules. If something went differently than planned, who would know about it? Of course, Kevin couldn't resist being the joker.

"Your project manager would be the first to know that you are MIA since you talk three to five times a day to help keep the project on course!"

I laughed, but it got me thinking. Who would know? I knew that God was always watching over me, but how would my family know? I couldn't imagine never seeing their beautiful faces again.

At that point in our work as traveling electronic health record consultants, Kevin usually worked in one location for a few weeks before he moved to a new destination. I was out traveling weekly all over the country helping 83 hospitals implement electronic health records. Sometime I went to three different locations in a 5-day period.

I spent the next day working at the hospital in San Angelo before driving to Dallas. Dallas was 320 miles away, but at 80 mph, it only took four hours. The following morning I would get on an airplane and fly from Dallas to Seattle, Washington, and then on to Anchorage, Alaska.

At the Hampton Inn in Dallas, I prepared for the long day of travel. I repacked so I would not have to check any luggage. The flight to Alaska was seven hours of flying time, so I made sure I packed a book in my briefcase.

Speaking of books, I also began to think about writing a book. In the past, many people had asked me to write down my spiritual journey so they could read it and share it with their friends. I never had the desire to write a novel, but I did want our children to have access to the incredible journey God rolled out for our lives. Of course, I also wanted to share with our friends.

The book in my briefcase was a small red paperback I had been carrying around for months. I had previously cracked the cover and read a few pages but never got beyond that. My love for reading non- fiction books began years before we had our children. As a child, I loved to write about my spiritual journey with Jesus Christ. In the business of life and lack of time, the reading habit had become lax, and the writing habit had certainly gone out the window.

With all that was going on in my life, the idea of writing a book my children could enjoy in the future seemed like a huge undertaking, and I was not sure if I was up to the challenge. Still, people kept asking me to write a book. Therefore, I had two potential audiences: my children and the people around me who wanted to read about my spiritual journey. But, did I have anything to say? Would people really want to read what I wrote? And why now? As I learned, sometimes it was not up to us to decide. Sometimes, our actions are guided by Another.

I boarded my plane on Tuesday morning, got situated in my seat, and slept for a while. After some time, I awoke and thought *I have work to do*! But another voice inside said *Make time to read. I must make time to read*.

Reading was a great source for helping me to grow stronger in every avenue of my life. The spiritual, the mental, professional, financial, and relational aspects of life were categories in which I knew I needed to be stretching myself. I cracked the little red cover book and read a few pages, and continued to read and continued to read all the while telling myself I had work to do. I knew I would always have work, but somehow I needed to learn to make time for the things that were going to help me grow into a better person, mother, wife, sister, and friend.

Before the end of the next flight, I had finished reading the book. That little red book called *The Greatest Salesman in the World Part II* was the pushing point that got me to pen these words. Some would have called it coincidence, but I called it divine intervention. The Lord for some reason had put many people in my path to encourage me to write, but I wasn't listening at the time. It took quite an emotional experience running on empty in a desolate area of Texas for me to listen.

Of course, by the time I finished reading the book, I didn't need another clue as to what I needed to do. I knew I must begin writing our journey to share the intervention of God's hand in our lives. I needed to shout to the world "We have been Blessed!"

I knew that most people never took the time in the hassle and business of the world to reflect on the things that happened in their lives, and the Lord knew I was one of those people. I was a mother of four children and the wife of one incredible man. He knew when he married me that life was going to be an adventurous journey with many destinations along the way.

I wrote this book while flying all over the country working as a healthcare IT consultant. Those duties took me from my usual tasks of being a mother and an owner of a real estate business. My consulting week consisted of several flights, meetings with executives of hospitals all over the country, and workflow analysis to help prepare the facilities for the implementation of their electronic health records.

I tried to understand. Why now Lord? I work a hundred hours a week and You want me to write a book? What? Really, what do I have to share and why is it so important? *I* didn't know, but I was going to be obedient to His wishes, so I wrote.

Kevin and I had lived our lives in a manner that didn't make sense to our human minds, but I knew God's plan was divine. God revealed himself through a willing soul, a vessel. I was just trying to be that vessel. If I did as he asked, the vessel would continue to overflow.

# Chapter 2

## Is This Real?

That morning I awoke to a bright sunrise peaking over the mountains in Anchorage, packed my bag, fixed my hair, put make up on, and ran out the door to turn my car in at the rental counter. I grabbed a coffee and waited to board my flight, once again sitting in awe of the One who made it all possible. A few minutes later, I boarded my flight and sat in the back of the plane where the single passengers usually were seated. But today someone had different plans for me.

I sat next to a young girl in her late teens and her mother who looked about 35. I could tell from my many years as a nurse, and the oxygen cannula in her nose, that her mother was probably terminally ill. After exchanging some pleasantries, I learned they were traveling from Alaska to Virginia to visit some family. They were very quiet and reserved during the flight, and were both embarrassed at the many times they had to ask me to move so the mother could get to the restroom.

At first I was agitated because it was so early in the morning and I wanted to try to get some additional sleep, but then I thought that this could just as easily have been my nine-year old daughter, Kora, and me in that situation. I thought about the premature journey those two were sharing in the last years of the mother's life. My attitude turned to a mindful moment of prayer and consideration for all God had provided for my family and me. He had blessed us with friends, fun, forgiveness, and good health. As I began to reflect, I asked for forgiveness for my agitation when the mother had needed to go to the restroom.

Then I had one of the strangest thoughts I had ever had while flying. I had had my share of flights by this time, and even with all my medical training, I had never I thought about what I would do if there were a medical emergency or a death on a flight. The young girl and her mother made me realize that sick people travel too. That realization was that God was preparing me for the journey ahead.

Our flight arrived early into Seattle Washington, and I hoped mother and daughter made it to their final destination safely. The biggest thing on my mind was making it home and meeting up with my dear friend Amy. I checked the departure board and saw I could catch an earlier flight home - the problem was it left in 15 minutes. No time for lunch! I wanted to see if I could make that flight in order to spend more time with someone in whose life I was trying to invest.

"You know there will be a $75 change fee, don't you?" the gate attendant asked me without looking up.

I was still out of breath from running to the gate. "Are there seats available?" I asked between gasps for air.

She didn't answer. "Ticket please."

I handed it over to her, ready to be disappointed or ready to pay $75. Seeing Amy early was worth way more than $75, but something else told me I needed to be on that flight.

The attendant didn't speak; she just took my ticket and looked at the numbers.

I don't know what happened. Next thing I knew, my name was first on the standby list, and there was no charge. Nothing! "Thanks," I managed to say as I walked through the gate. I shook my head and didn't give it anymore thought since my goal was to get back to Longview, Texas and spend the evening having some relaxation and girl time with Amy.

Just then, my cell phone rang. It was one of my mentors and we chatted until it was time to turn off our electronic devices. Of course, I got a seat in the back and boarded the plane, happy to be able to reconnect with my dear friend sooner. Due to the circumstances, I had skipped lunch and my stomach and everyone else were aware. Once in flight, I asked the attendant for a snack box if possible. I went to hand him my Visa card and he noticed my driver's license was from Michigan. He asked where I lived and we chatted briefly. Of course, there was no charge for my lunch. I began to think about all the things that had just gone on in the last hour. *Why me Lord? Why have I been so blessed?* I was not complaining, and I was not upset by this, but just moved! Had I really done so much to have this kind of favor on my life? I felt so unworthy and I was grateful to be blessed beyond measure. Thank you Jesus for dying on the cross so that I could be a vessel in the world for Your Kingdom.

I rested a while on the jet since the day was going to be long and the time with Amy meant so much to me that I didn't want to be exhausted. Then I awoke and was just thinking and pondering about the things in my life. All at once, the overhead speaker announced, "if there is a nurse or a doctor on the plane please put your call light on." What other option do I have Lord? None! I immediately placed my call light on and a flight attendant ushered me to the front of the plane.

There was an elderly woman and her daughter traveling together and she was not feeling well. By this time, I was not the only medical professional that showed up to the scene - a surgeon, and another nurse were already there attempting to care for the patient. Of course, it seemed to me like they waited to come help until someone else offered to help, but that is a story for another time.

They decided to put the woman on the floor as if to begin CPR, but the woman was alert and able to speak to us.

"She has no pulse!" the doctor cried out. He then stated the obvious, "She's not doing well!"

I had been a nurse for 17 years, an EMT, worked in the Emergency Department, and delivered babies for a living; however, due to all the commotion, I felt useless in the situation. I asked the daughter a few questions, then I said, "I used to be an emergency room nurse, but I feel like there isn't room for me to do anything but assist now." I felt terribly awkward and useless as I looked into her tear-filled eyes. As if it were some consolation, I added, "I wasn't even supposed to be on this flight!"

She looked at me and grabbed the crosses on my necklace and said "Oh yes you were!" She held onto the crosses as if they were her link to the Father.

"All I can offer you is prayer," I replied. We closed our eyes and I prayed for the mother and her daughter. "Amen," I concluded.

"Amen," she echoed. "I know your prayer will be answered. Thank God you were on this flight."

The Doctor decided an emergency landing would be best at this time. We landed in Albuquerque and the woman was taken off the flight alive by the emergency crew that met us on the runway.

As I returned to my seat and thought about the day's happenings, I listened to those around me complaining and griping about how their travel plans had changed and their trips were going to be messed up. What a shame that this was their mentality when there was someone in need.

I had plans that evening with a very dear friend too, but enough was enough. The Lord had other plans and I was called to be His vessel at that time. I didn't know the name of the mother or the daughter from that situation, but it doesn't matter. God needed me to show up in their lives at that moment for reasons far greater than I will ever know. Living life on Purpose.

As I ponder that day's events it became clearer and clearer to me how one change in the course of life's events can truly change the course of the world. If I would have counted the number of people on the plane whose lives were affected, it would have been well over 150 and their lives being impacted meant many others were as well.

While others were grumbling and complaining, I was growing and preparing for the future. Everything we have done in our past prepares us for the very moment we are in. God has been preparing me for so long and I have tried to be a hungry student to learn every day and seek His counsel and for guidance in our lives. The course of the week's events had truly revealed the many challenges that have been put before me as preparation for incredible things to come. How many people can actually hear and see God speak directly to their soul? I believe everyone can but you must be the willing vessel.

I spent some time thinking and recreating the moments in my mind. Was it a dream? How did I get here? Why me? If the events that day were puzzle pieces, they would not have fit as neatly into a puzzle if I had designed it myself. Think of the possibility of something that could occur and rehearsing in my mind what I would do should a situation actually play out and then hours later the very event being laid out before my eyes. It was like dress rehearsal. I am still in awe!

I could not have had a clearer direction from God in my life that it was time to start drafting some of what you are reading now.

# Chapter 3

## The Past Shapes the Future

Our journey began many years ago when Christ brought Kevin and me together in nursing school. We met very early on at the University and seemed always to be "placed" together. At the time, I could have cared less - he was one of 10 guys in a class of 120 girls and I knew he would never date me or I him. I was just there for school, and I had no interest in making or building friendships with anyone there. I was a small town girl and intended to stay a small town girl the rest of my life. Of course, God had different plans for both of us.

Kevin had lived his entire life in what I called the city. He claimed it was not the city, so we differed on this. If there was a grocery store within a couple miles, that was city to me. Kevin had a different perspective, but I was writing the book, so grocery store equaled city.

Of course, every girl who wasn't already in a relationship was in love with Kevin. I thought he was attractive, but he wore clean work boots to class. Who did that? In my world, work boots were for the barn, and I would not wear them out for public display.

Two years later, Kevin and I met up at a nursing student party. We played a Michigan card game and won almost every hand that night. We were having fun just hanging out as friends, and I happened to mention that my boyfriend, I had broken up, and I was on a kissing strike. I had a bad taste in my mouth from the previous relationship. I thought I should take some time and get through nursing school, and then maybe I would worry about looking for my soul mate.

Kevin walked me out to my car and dared me to kiss him. I am from small town America and I just thought that was crazy since we were there with everyone we had gone to school with. Who does that? The crazier part was I asked to come to my apartment to have coffee. At the time, I lived with six girls and I knew Kevin well enough that this was probably a safe move. I found him very interesting and was of course attracted to many things about him. We talked for a few more hours and I was anxiously waiting for him to kiss me, and he was waiting for the coffee to be made. By the way, he didn't even drink coffee before he met me. The crazy little things we do to impress others. We have both enjoyed kissing and coffee ever since.

It was only a couple days into seeing each other on a more serious basis that he asked me to go church with him. WAIT!!! I was the one who always asked the guy to go to church with me. My heart leaped for joy! I knew in my heart this was the one God had prepared for me. Kevin knew too and we went to look for wedding rings before Thanksgiving. It was exciting and I loved spending as much time with him as I could, and of course we shared a lot of coffee and kisses.

We each had one semester left in school and we were driving 45 mins each way to see each other. In addition, Kevin was very busy with his social life. I quickly found that I didn't fit there. He knew I felt awkward as well, but he wasn't sure how to handle the circumstances. As I look back now, we went through a lot just to be with each other the first year. Only by God's plan did we marry and grow so close. Of course, we were complete opposites and still didn't have everything in our marriage figured out, except one thing – Commitment to God, each other, and our children.

Kevin loved to hang out with his friends and participate in unhealthy activities. I told him within months of being together if he chose to live that way, then I was not going to be part of his life. Fortunately, for me he chose to make some changes in his life and he gave up things he had known for a long time. Please don't think he is not a good man because I am sharing this here. I am sharing so one of you can know and understand that with Christ all things are possible. Kevin knew the way he should be living, but he had had very little guidance in his life from those who should have provided it. Over many tears, coffee, kisses and prayers Kevin was freed from much bondage in his life. This took time and acceptance by me. I loved Kevin but hated some of the activities he wanted to participate in.

Finally one day I said, "I want no part of it, and if you want to be with me you will have to give up those behaviors!"

"I understand, Toni," was all Kevin could offer at the time.

I want to disclose that acceptance does not mean approval. It just means trying to love someone regardless of where they are in their journey. I was very hurt by the behavior and confused as to why it was fun. I thought it was pure destruction. I must have seemed pushy and bossy to him and his friends when I didn't want to play the game. But I had been down the road before with things that led to a lot of hurt in my life and I didn't like living with guilt. When Kevin decided to move on it took a long time for him to apologize to me for the activities. This showed how much love and respect Kevin had for me and that he was guilt-ridden after years of being away from that lifestyle.

When you choose to "give up" to "go up," it usually means you will be giving up the friends who held you in bondage as well. For a guy that can be a difficult thing to surrender and he knew before the wedding the friends he shared for a long time were not going to be our friends for long. The part that saddens me is that Kevin had been so actively involved with the church and his family attended on a regular basis, yet where was the Lord's guidance in his life? I didn't understand the lack of control and influence that should have been in his life from a very early age. The family talked and they had holidays together, but nothing beyond the surface was ever brought up.

Why did some people live such fake lives? Lord, I pray to help me be real with people, admit my faults, grow, and learn to become better. I thank The Lord Jesus for all the relationships that have been built into my life that I could go deep with, often over coffee and kisses.

I was not wise beyond my years when I was young, I just have never believed in wasting time. Kevin and I knew each other for all of nursing school and began dating in the final year. I was in a few serious relationships prior to Kevin, and I was even engaged. So, there were some qualifications I put on the table not long after we started dating each other. I simply told him if he didn't know if he wanted to marry me after a year of dating, then I would be history. I didn't want to invest too much time with one person if he wasn't willing to make a commitment to me. I was and still am a motivated person striving to move constantly forward in life, which meant for me I didn't want to be in a long relationship without knowing I was investing time into a lifelong commitment. We laugh now because we can talk about our courting period and Kevin confessed to me that he had never even thought about getting married until we began dating. He probably only thought about marriage because I was the one who brought it up. This just goes to show the difference in the reason I was dating and the reason he was dating.

About ten months after our first date, Kevin I and got into a huge fight and I told him I didn't want to see him anymore. I can still remember insisting he go home and not come back to see me. His behavior in my mind was unacceptable. He left and we went three days without talking to each other. I still do not know how I survived. I remember wanting to pick up the phone and call him so badly. I remember feeling like half of me was missing, but I just would not allow myself to be hurt anymore by his immature behavior. When I broke off my engagement a couple years earlier, I can remember telling my former fiancé, it wasn't that I didn't love him, but that I wasn't in love with him. Sure, I could have married someone I could live with, but I wanted to marry someone I felt I could not live without. There was a big difference there, and when you truly felt you didn't want to live without someone, then you may have just found the one you should spend the rest of time with. That would take a lot of coffee and kisses to discover though. What I had learned in my past shaped what I wanted my future to look like, and for once, I was smart enough to remember that.

Of course, we made up, and then things were different. I didn't know how or why things changed, but maybe a trigger flipped in Kevin's mind that I would really leave and we wouldn't be together if things weren't different. I knew during those three days of us being separated he went and bought me a ring. He never mentioned it or said he made the trip, but I could sense there would soon be a day he would propose.

He told me he wanted to go to Toronto to see the Phantom of the Opera and take a little time away. I agreed and allowed him to make the arrangements. The show was fantastic! And of course, he had picked out an area with a fountain to take me to after the show. He got down on one knee and asked me to marry him. I told him I loved him. He said he knew that but wanted to know if I would marry him. I think it took him three times to ask me before I answered him with what he was looking for. We were both so excited and could hardly wait to get back home to tell everyone.

The closer the wedding got, the more the excitement built. We bought a home and prepared it to live in when we returned from our honeymoon. We had long talks about the future and goals we wanted to achieve together, over coffee and kisses. I still remember like a sword piercing through my soul when I heard these words come out of his mouth.

Kevin said to my mother's husband, "I learned how to shave on my own, how to change the oil in my car, how to fix things around the house, but I have had no one to teach me how to be a husband or a father."

This has stirred my soul for years and been what I call the biggest challenge of our marriage. He was begging for a mentor and a coach in his life, and no one showed up. How sad, but what qualifies anyone for the role?

I believe it can be summed up in the three "As" – Accept, Approve, and Appreciate. First, each partner must accept the other one for who they are, not who they want them to be. Second, each must approve of the way each partner is behaving in the relationship. Finally, each partner must appreciate what the other is doing for the relationship. A bond must be built and if a friendship or a relationship cannot be formed, it is often because one of the three steps mentioned above has been skipped.

# Chapter 4

## Finding a Mentor

Fortunately for us, The Lord had given us favor from very early on in our marriage. When I was in my first year of nursing school at the university, I applied for a scholarship without realizing how much of an impact that decision would have on the rest of my and our family's lives. Dr. John Ylvisaker will go down in history as one of the Barnett family hero's for all he taught us and shared. He was a medical doctor, a surgeon and a very business-minded gentleman. After medical school, he married a young woman from the upper peninsula of Michigan. Her name was Tekla. Once they married and settled in Bloomfield Hills, Michigan, they had four children, a young boy and shortly thereafter a set of triplets. It was a busy time for them, but this didn't stop Dr. Y from continuing to pursue a fantastic medical career and an adventurous life in the real estate market.

At much too young of an age, Tekla was diagnosed with cancer. When Tekla passed away, Dr. Y set up a scholarship program through the local university in honor of his dear lovely wife. This wasn't just a scholarship program like ones I had received many previous times through God's blessing in my life, but a real mentor ship program. What? And he was going to pay me? It really didn't make sense at all to me nor did I understand what I was getting into when I applied. I soon learned that Dr. Y wanted to build a true relationship with the scholarship winner and make an impact in the lives of the recipients through influence. He wasn't interested in control, but realized the significance of influence lasting long after he would physically be in this world.

Dr. Y took it upon himself to perform the interviews of each candidate once the school narrowed down the search. I really had no idea what to expect when I went for the interview. I walked in the door and Dr. Y asked, "tell me about yourself." At that time it was easy because I had done little reading or had little coaching in my life, so I thought it was all about me. I talked about myself for 45 mins, and I got up and left. I had no idea what went wrong and immediately called my mom. "He only asked one question!" I was sure that would be the last I heard about the scholarship.

Before I could park my car in the driveway, I received a call from the University. We would like to let you know Dr. Y has selected you to be the candidate for this year's scholarship. For real? I thought I messed it all up.

That was amazing. They had an introductory banquet at the Palace in Auburn Hills for me and the journey began. Dr. Y and I became very close very quickly. He became the grandfather I never had and the man who listened and never judged but offered sound advice when he thought I needed it in a very gentle loving manner. We would often talk about the day of the interview and how he was taken back when I bounced into the room. He was expecting me to be a male, and when I surprised him and immediately reminded him of Tekla, I won! He said he wasn't sure if he ever heard a word I said because he already knew I was going to be given the next award.

Our relationship grew and blossomed because of the time he wanted to invest in me. Growing up in a small town, I had never dreamed of the things he exposed me to. Dinners that cost more than most people make in a day, airplane rides with him as the pilot and four wheeler rides with me driving down backcountry roads. We shared laughs, tears, and heartbreaks. We influenced each other's lives in ways many people have no idea about to this day. He knew I loved horses and when he built his new home, he asked me to come and let him know what I thought about the layout and where the horse barn should be. How was I the chosen one? To this day, I know this was all part of God great plan for all the things to come.

Dr. Y challenged me to dream and taught me some very valuable lessons. Think about how you can live if you are willing to step outside the box a little. He exposed me to a lifestyle that I knew was possible because he did it.

The basic principle he taught me was: Define, Learn, Do. Dr. Y helped me begin my define process and was willing to teach until the day he passed on. He gave back to the people who surrounded him every day of his life. He lived to his nineties and his calendar was full all the time, but never once did he not make room for me. If I invited him somewhere he was there, if I needed to talk, he took the call, when I needed a pick me up, he sent a note. The example and handprint he left on our lives was beyond measure.

When Dr. Y was in residency, he bought and renovated apartments to earn passive cash flow. He drove older cars and worked on the homes after hospital hours. He began with the end in mind, and was willing to work hard knowing what he was doing today others would not do, so someday he could do what others could not do. We often talked and laughed about how other physicians laughed at him and his ideas: working after work, and buying 100 acres in Clarkston, Michigan. Who did that crazy stuff? What they couldn't see was the dream he had. He went on to own many apartments, shopping complexes, mini storages, golf courses, snow and lawn service businesses, and condos. He developed sub divisions where one parcel sold covered his entire investment cost. He owned sailboats, airplanes, multiple homes, cars, horses, pools, etc. What for? Because he could. But never for one minute was it all for him. He shared and loaned things out, threw parties and took people to dinner and built relationships. He had learned that people were his greatest assets, and he wanted to build into their lives knowing it was going to enrich his. I loved him dearly and he is greatly missed.

Kevin and Dr. Y hit it off immediately and it was no surprise when we announced our engagement. I believe he was more shocked when we asked him to speak at our wedding than the actual engagement. He was good at public speaking and others enjoyed listening to him tell his stories. He shared some of our experiences and made the day super special for us. When we decided to buy our first home just a few short miles from him, he was dead set against it and told us to reconsider. Just take some time to get to know each other and be married. We didn't take his advice and purchased the house anyway as it was well within our means and we couldn't see renting. It didn't take long for Dr. Y to come to us and apologize for what he said. I see now this was a very smart move for the two of you and I am glad you made this choice. We spent many days and afternoons at his pool, playing, laughing, and talking about real estate. We told him we wanted to buy a house in Pontiac to renovate and rent. Of course he couldn't agree more with our decision. We borrowed forty thousand dollars from the bank. Then we purchased a house for $25 thousand and put the balance of the money into the renovation process.

Every spare minute, Kevin and I worked together on the house. Dr. Y visited often to check our progress, and I began to see qualities that I didn't know existed in Kevin. He was incredible with his hands, and if I could put the vision together, he could make it become reality. We learned a lot about each other that summer. We had a bit of a different outlook on construction than most people do. Nurses hold people's lives in the palm of their hand every day, and we knew if we made a wrong or bad nursing decision it would affect someone's health or that of a loved one. Construction was different. If it didn't work the first time, we could tear it out and redo it, and if it looked bad, no one was going to die from it. We quickly rented the house, and we were not sure how we felt about being landlords. It was a learning experience for us, and the beginning of learning to be a team and help each other to succeed.

I saw Kevin get mad for the first time. I wasn't sure he had that in him, but it was there and just took a lot to push him to the edge. We worked together constantly. Not only were we working at the same hospital together, but also we were investing every waking hour we had into this house. One day, I wanted him to hang a light in the dining room and he had other plans for the day. Of course, I continued to push him to hang the light. I now realize he was trying to make me happy, but he really only wanted to follow his own agenda for the day and it didn't include hanging a chandelier. He must have tried to put the light up nine times and every time something wasn't right. He finally got angry and lost his temper, but it took a lot for him to get there. I am grateful for a man who is slow to anger. Another blessing to count over coffee and kisses.

We experienced the same kind of things Dr. Y told us would happen. No one else understood why we would want to work our summer away on that old house. For one thing, it gave us a goal to accomplish together, and for the second thing, we saw it as a way to earn some extra money. We rented the home for two years for $900 per month and then sold it for $72 thousand. Not a bad ROI when we really didn't have a clue what we were doing. Dr. Y was so proud and we often spoke about how we could move forward and better leverage ourselves.

# Chapter 5

## Dream, Struggle, Victory

In the fall after we finished the home, we received a weird phone message on our answering machine. We returned the call and next thing we know we were on our way to a networking marketing meeting. We were so excited as we had finally discovered a way to do the work once and get paid over and over. Lord knows we were not afraid of the work. This was a different adventure, and we thought we were going to be multimillionaires in this business. We contacted everyone we knew and plugged into every bit of information we could. The networking industry was phenomenal for teaching timeless principles. We shut off our television and began to read books. We devoured books. Where had this information been all our lives? Why had no one ever told us any of what seemed like logical principles? We began to see how these principles lined directly up with what the Bible teaches. It was amazing to us. We became very close with a team of people that we worked with and tried to fight and win the battle together. We learned principles that applied to many methods: relationship building, adherence to business principles, developing leadership skills, visualization of dreams, and the list goes on.

Unfortunately, despite our best efforts, the business fell apart due to leadership issues and product changes. That was in 2007, and we weren't sure what we were going to do. We just knew we weren't ready to give up on passive income, not yet. The seeds of greatness had been planted years before when we met people who allowed us to see them up close and personal. They revealed themselves as who they were and not what they had. Kevin and I learned there was a process to becoming the people to attract the things we dreamt about. We learned you couldn't take your crappy old self into a bright new future, so we became and we are still becoming.

# Chapter 6

## A Growing Family

From the very first cup of coffee we ever shared, Kevin knew I wanted to stay home to raise our children. This was a big dream, considering that we had done very well financially, but had nothing to show for it. We were paid well and spent well. Yes, life was fun but when we found out we were pregnant with our first-born we were truly not prepared to lose half our income.

The blessings that Kora brought into our lives, and the joy of watching my husband become a loving father, were priceless. That little girl meant so many things to so many people, not just to us but also to those around her who knew and loved her. But could we live on half our family's income? Would we be able to afford diapers? Could we still go out to dinner? What about a babysitter if we wanted to go out?

When I quit my job, we had less than ten grand in the bank. Of course, The Lord provided for us and we leveraged money just to live and pay for some of the necessary items in life. We enjoyed our lives and didn't even realize we were creating a financial nightmare if we continued down that path.

To show how oblivious we were to our situation, nine months postpartum we decided to try to have another baby since our dream was to have the children close together in age. About a year later, we were blessed with little Kendra. Our family had now doubled in size, but our bank account was shrinking at an alarming rate. We were too enamored with our new family to notice though. As always though, God was watching over us.

# Chapter 7

## Challenges Within and Without

That was difficult for me to write about, but it actually fit into another valuable lesson. I knew that people made decisions based on emotion, not intellect. A man convinced against his will was of the same opinion still. When something stirs a person's soul, he will either cognitively make a choice to change or to remain unmoved by the event. Since our decisions are usually based on emotion, when we looked back logically, things didn't always add up.

Kendra was a challenging baby: she was up every two hours around the clock for 11 months. I was tired, but I still enjoyed the journey. We were still desperately trying to get the networking business to work for us, but we felt more like we were just putting a bandage on it. We had tons of coffee with people and worked on building relationships. But we felt like failures because we had worked so long, had invested so much money, and had spent so much time trying to reach the goal without success. What we could not see at that time was that The Lord was preparing us for the real journey ahead. We continued to beat the pavement, read books, grew trying to adjust ourselves, became more flexible, and learned that life was about the journey and not the end. It required many cups of coffee and tons of kisses now too.

The girls, Kora and Kendra were small, but the little two bedroom home was beginning to drive me crazy. There was constantly stuff everywhere and nowhere to put it. One Sunday afternoon, my girlfriend Linda came over to hang out. I asked her if she wanted to stroll over to an open house up the road. We put the kids in the strollers and took a walk. We stepped into the house and met Ms. T (Tanya, but my kids will always call her Ms. T) and momma Pearl. Tanya was the real estate agent holding the open house, and she showed us through the home and we talked. Linda and I both liked the house, and I liked the idea of having a friend move closer to us, but she and her husband decided not to pursue that home and stay where they were. But I was curious now. Ms. T and I talked about the possibility of selling our home to buy something else.

"Oh," she said, "you live in the cute little blue house up the street? I am sure we could sell that and help you find something else."

I called Kevin, and asked, "What do you think about putting the house up for sale?"

"I don't care," was all he could manage.

We listed the house on Tuesday over a cup of coffee in our dining room. Now please remember this was in 2007 when the market in Michigan was beginning to fall apart. Ms. T began to send us listings of homes in our price range. Of course, we found a beautiful ranch style house with a fabulous lot and a walkout basement and a two-car garage and space for the kids to play. It needed some work, but we weren't afraid of that. Lord, I thought, how can this work? We can't have two house payments. Please help us sell our home so we can move.

The ranch house was vacant, and the girls and I would often take drives out there to sit on the back porch where we prayed and dreamt that someday we could live there. It seemed like we went every day, but that was probably an exaggeration. But I understood you got what you pictured, and we were picturing ourselves living there. Sometimes we would sing, and dance, and cry and share kisses over the experience of just being there. We didn't understand the how or any details; we just focused on the dream. You see your mind will figure out the details until you tell it things won't work. Why do people drive cars they can't pay for? Because the mind has figured out the how even when it doesn't make logical sense.

Ms. T showed our home and she was trying everything she could to get it sold, but it was just a slow time in real estate due to the economy. Then, one Monday morning in early Oct I received a dreadful phone call from my father, "Toni, my big blue barn burnt to the ground last night."

"What? I am on my way dad!" I called my mom and told her I was coming up to cook some food so I could take it over to dad during this tragic time for him. I pulled in the driveway of my mom's house and my phone rang.

"Tanya here. Just calling to let you know there has been an offer placed on the home you want to buy. The weird thing is the lady who will make the decision on the offer is out of the office until Thursday so you will have until Thursday to decide what you want to do."

"Oh, wonderful!" I burst out in tears. "For real Lord? Why today?" How was I going to tell my little girls the dream was shattered? Over coffee and kisses?

No, I was not going to tell them the dream was over, God doesn't work that way. I was going to tell them we needed to pray harder and ask for the answer. God would give us the desires of our heart. I explained to the tiny ears what had just happened. Even though they were only three and eighteen months, they understood tears meant sadness and prayer could fix things.

Anyhow, that day wasn't about us. Papa needed us and we needed to move our selfishness out of the way. We went inside and explained to grandma what had happened and asked for prayer for everyone all the way around. We prepared a meal and delivered it to Papa about 15 miles up the road. Dad was glad to see us all. We shared some tears, dinner, kisses, and coffee. I drove home that night with my little angels praying for an answer about the house. My soul was sad, but I wasn't willing to quit yet.

# Chapter 8

## Dream Struggle Victory II

I explained to Kevin all the events of the day. He knew the desires of our hearts too.

"How about we rent our house out? I am sure we can cover the payment and we won't have to change our finances, he said with hope in his voice. "See what you can do."

I think I was up half the night looking through craigslist to see what I thought I could rent the house for and how long we could go financially if the rent wasn't paid.

By Thursday evening, I had someone who wanted to rent the house; this would cover the payment and give us $100 per month positive cash flow. It will work Lord. Thanks again for the safety net.

I must have talked to Tanya 30 times that week. But she never one time acted annoyed or frustrated by our many calls and questions. She was glad to write our offer for only $100 over the asking price since we wanted the home so badly.

By Friday morning, we knew they had accepted our offer and we signed the lease on our house on Saturday morning. I began to pack boxes, pick out furniture and gather paint swatches. The girls had so much fun in this process. They loved gathering paint swatches and Formica pieces at Home Depot. Don't think for one minute that this was easy. You have never met Kendra, and if you ever get the blessing of meeting Ms. T, she will give you the true reality of what life was like with that child. But The Lord removed those memories for good reason.

Kevin asked mom and dad to help us with the renovation process and explained that we would live in the basement while we worked on the house until it was finished. I loved having my mom there to help me with choices and the work. We were often working until the wee hours of the morning. We had home renovations of 2000 square feet to finish. We quickly learned that working with two small children was a ton of work. The girls needed my time and the work needed to be finished. Sleep was highly overrated. With the help of my dear parents, we finished the home in 6 weeks and moved upstairs. The furniture was delivered and Christmas was a joyous celebration.

This was the beginning of our girls seeing you get what you picture, and to this day, they just believe if you pray for it, it happens. They have more faith in their young years of life than I could ever have imagined was possible. To have the faith of a child....

We settled in and had Ms. T over to see the house. She was amazed at the changes we had made to the home in such a short time. We felt very close to her for helping us make our dream come true. She brought a house-warming gift and we shared some coffee and kisses in the "new" dining room. She loved it as we did, and it will always have a very special place in our hearts. She was just amazed at how beautifully the work had been done and the way we worked together with our parents to accomplish this goal.

"You guys should fix up homes as a business," she offered. "I come across many homes that could benefit from your skill in renovations."

Kevin and I talked about that idea briefly, but we had so many things going on in our lives, we let it drop quickly. Our two small girls adored us, and we enjoyed them so much, we hated to embark on something that would reduce the time we spent with them. We were also still trying to decide what to do about the networking business now that the leadership was going down a different road. We were just hanging out, still looking to fulfill the dream.

# Chapter 9

## The Next Road to Travel

Spring came before we knew it, and the economy was just getting worse. People were leaving their homes, losing their jobs, and having to move on due to untold circumstances. I look back now and sometimes still don't understand why we felt so blessed, but nonetheless, we did. It was not as we were wealthy, but broke can be a state of mind. We always paid all our bills and sometimes had a little extra. We were not rolling in the cash though.

The little house we rented out the previous fall was going to need to be reconstructed because the tenants thought they owned the house and were renovating it on their own. They had no idea what they were doing and the place was a disaster. Without so much as lifting a paintbrush, we put a FOR RENT sign in the front yard after Ms. T educated me about the rental market. We received about 50 phone calls to rent the house in the next 6 days. Kevin and I were blown away by this. So many people wanted to rent that little house that was actually in pieces.

I showed the house to potential tenants while the home was under construction and explained to them how things would look. I also asked them if they would be interested in selecting some of the features that would be added to the house. Paint colors, light fixtures, carpet styles, backsplash tile etc. Our little team: Kevin, Ms. T, the girls, and I thought it was a fabulous idea! A business model where we could allow the customer to have a choice...WOW! What a concept.

Meanwhile, I was so excited about this process and the journey we were on, I told my parents they should buy some houses and fix them up to rent, lease, land contract, or sell. Of course, mom loved the idea, but dad not so much. But they embarked on the journey with a house that was somewhat roughed in and made it stunning.

After we completed the renovations on the house, we began looking at other properties. We found a small house for $35,000. It needed work, but that didn't bother us. Ms. T walked into the house and walked out when she showed it to us. She couldn't believe we were going to buy it and kept telling us it was a lot of work, but she was not going to change our minds. We cleaned out our saving account and applied for a loan through a broker we knew could help us. We towed the girls with us every day and worked from dawn until dark. Kevin crawled through spiders and mud to replace the plumbing. The girls quickly made friends with the neighbors. We prayed for The Lord to bless the house and bring us a good tenant.

There was time for lots of cleaning, painting, dry walling, replacing flooring, tiling, gardening, and adding our signature finishing touches. The Lord blessed us with a tenant before we were finished with the renovations. Ms. T was very impressed once again with our ability to work as a team and accomplish so much in a short amount of time with the girls participating every day. Our dream was that no matter what path The Lord led us down, our children would be included in it. We always wanted to make them our priority and we discussed that often over coffee and kisses.

One principle we learned while active in the networking business was to sit down and write out our dreams. We did this and did it often. Then we talked about it, just as it was going to come true. We often went and looked at things we couldn't afford knowing that someone else had made the way for themselves to be able to afford those things. It was not because we had to have those things, but that it was possible and it was motivation to us. We also learned that often times those who have made it to what

Kiyosaki calls the 5% world have often had to help a lot of people along the way.

The principle here is to enjoy the journey. Often the destination is not as one perceives it will be, and materialistic items are not a bad thing if they help to motivate us to become better people. Remember: Dream, Struggle, Victory. The struggle is usually where people quit. What most of us don't realize is that when it gets hard, we are growing. Do more and get better! We find out just how much we can actually accomplish when we realize we are on the same team and we aren't sitting around watching TV.

# Chapter **10**

## Clouds in the Coffee

Since one home renovation worked for my parents, and one worked for us that summer, we talked about starting a business together to fix up homes. My step dad had lost his job and was a general contractor and very good with construction. I loved working with my mom and creating new ideas. My mom was nervous.

"I really want to be able to do this with you guys, but I don't want this to ruin the relationship we have with you," she said.

I reassured her it would not and suggested we take a chance. Up until this point, we had spent a ton of time with my parents working on our networking business and my mom loved the girls as if they were her own children, I loved this. Kevin adored my parents and we really enjoyed having them around. We spent many hours over coffee figuring out how this was going to work and where we would get money. Of course, dad recommended we talk to Dr. Y to see if he would like to become a silent investor in our company.

We invited Dr. Y to the house for dinner. I made his favorite meal, meatloaf, and we shared our dreams with him over coffee. He was impressed with what we wanted to accomplish. He believed it would work. But I still remember him telling us he never went into business with anyone. If he was going to do it, he was going to do it himself. He could not figure out why we would be coming to him and asking him to invest in our company when we had excellent credit and hadn't talked to the bank.

As I look back now, I am not sure why we didn't start with the bank either, but dad had his own way of wanting to do things. And so the trouble began. For the sake of their reputation, and my respect for my parents, I will not share that chapter in my life. We all still have open wounds in our minds and sores that have healed into scars.

There are things I still have not figured out, and I prayed to The Lord to help us to work through them. It just didn't make sense to me or those around us, but for some reason The Lord had pulled the window shade on those relationships and I didn't understand why. Kevin and I have had too many cups of coffee over this and probably not enough kisses.

# Chapter 11

## Increased Bounty through Connections

We knew we needed to buy more houses and increase our passive income using the principles of Dave Ramsey and Robert Kiyosaki. But how Lord? We were out of money and we knew things were not going well with the business with my parents. Pictures in our mind could make so many things happen. Many years ago, we saw where we wanted to be and knew we could get there, but we didn't know all the details. And we still didn't. We believed it could happen, and were willing vessels to do what it took to make it work.

We decided to go to a couple's conference in the spring. It was a blast! We laughed, shared, and enjoyed our time in Niagara Falls, Canada. We sat at a table with three other couples. Two couples were older than we were, and they had many great questions for us and offered some things that could help us with our business. One couple at the table was younger than we were. They had a lot of fun and listened intently to the conversations as we shared with the others about our real estate adventure.

By the end of the weekend, Eric and Andrea asked us for our number and said they would like to go to dinner and talk some more about how to get into the real estate market. We said that would be great and left the conference and drove home to Michigan. Once again, we did not know the journey we would be taking in the very near future.

# Chapter 12

## A Time for Building Friendships and the Beginning of a Legacy

The Lord knew we were going to need a business partner whose values and trust in the Lord would align with the way we lived our lives, which to the world often made no sense. We believed we should be in the world but not of the world, so we invested no time in caring about what others thought of us. We were not perfect, but we knew our judgement would be by Him and not by the Joneses. Who were the Joneses anyway?

We finally saw the upside of the business, and we were truly enjoying the journey together working all the time. We had two small girls, we were pregnant with another, we were managing multiple homes, and Kevin was working 4 days a week to get the debt paid down. We knew if we paid down the debt and lowered our expenses, we would be financially free sooner.

Linda called and asked if I would come to work for her one day a week at the hospital and do fetal non stress tests. I wasn't looking for a job, but I thought it would be fun to work a bit for some extra cash. Linda and I talked it over and decided Tuesday would be a good day since Kevin was always home on Tuesdays. I really only wanted to work so I could have some time to be with Linda. We had been friends a very long time, and I continually tried to invest into her life. It was a bit more difficult with her since she didn't like coffee and was not that fond of kisses either, but we had a fabulous friendship and she meant the world to me. She delivered all four of our babies and we would not have wanted to go through those blessed events without her.

We finished the renovation project and moved the tenant in. We began to look for another investment, praying that things would get better with my parents. We went to look at a house with mom and dad. Three out of the four of us wanted to put a bid in on it, but dad did not. He said he wasn't going to buy that house. The rest of us thought it was a good deal and didn't want to miss out on that one. I called Eric and asked if they wanted to go to dinner.

# Chapter 13

## Pre-Planned Events in our Life

We met with Eric and Andrea on a Friday evening, and we talked about what we had done and where we wanted to go. We told them we had looked at a house that morning and if they wanted to go look at it we could do that the next day. I was sure they walked into that house thinking *what are we doing here?* But we helped them see our vision and talked about how we could make this work for them, and how it would help us out. Once again, The Lord had prepared us for that moment.

On Monday, Eric and Andrea put an offer on the house and bought it with what we called creative financing. We all worked together on the house. That was part of the deal. They would learn about what we did and we would help them with every step of the process. The girls worked, Kevin worked, Andrea worked, Eric worked, and I worked. We had fun even though it was a lot of work. Many memories were made in that little house, many great memories, and many laughs. We shared so much, often over coffee and kisses. We all saw how an awesome team can work together and accomplish something great in a short amount of time. We helped them purchase that home for $31,000, and when we finished it a few short months later, it appraised for $109,000. I thought that was a good return on a house that my dad hadn't wanted to buy.

We were very pleased with our new friendship and were going to enjoy the winter recouping from a busy year. The baby was coming in November. Eric and Andrea were moving to Texas and that saddened my heart, but we knew God had far greater plans for them than they could have here.

I thank The Lord for willing vessels. You see the vessel showed up again just at the right time. They were willing, we were willing, and The Lord has continued to bless us all abundantly.

# Chapter 14

## The Innie and Outie

We were trying to get pregnant for a few months at the end of 2008 and into 2009. When I found out I was pregnant, Kevin was working on one of the houses with my mom putting cement block windows in. It was a cool wet spring day and he was outside working away with the concrete trying to mud the cement block windows in. I bent down over his shoulder and said, "We did it!"

"What?"

"We are going to have a baby!"

Even though he knew we were trying to conceive, he was still pleasantly surprised.

"Let's skip telling other people for a while, OK?" I offered.

"Of course, honey, anything you say," he replied as he went back to working with the cement.

Of course he couldn't keep it in, and mom knew before the end of the day, and so did Ms. T. The pregnancy was unremarkable, and we had no idea we were in for another miracle in our life.

We learned early in our marriage from the networking business that we needed to write things down as we saw them or the way we pictured them. Not in the circumstances we were in, but how they could be and how we wanted them to be. We had always dreamed of having four children, and God was preparing to give us number three in the next few months.

Prior to having children of our own, I was a labor and delivery nurse. I was blessed to be able to bring life into this world every day and watch God work right before me. Some people said miracles didn't happen anymore, but that was simply not true. Go work in the labor room of a busy hospital and you can be an eyewitness to the incredible works of The Lord. There were so many lives that were touched and impacted by the Power and the Grace of God, and sometimes those lives were hurting when human plans and God's plan didn't align.

The toughest thing in the world for a couple to go through is losing the life of a child, and often I was at the bedside. What do I say Lord? Where do I hide my tears when I am supposed to be the professional they are looking to for strength? I just allowed myself to rejoice with my patients when there were good times and hurt with them when things didn't feel right. I was human too.

Labor and Delivery was another time The Lord opened a door for me to be the vessel in people's lives. I loved the journey and during this time, God revealed to me how incredible it was to be part of someone's birth and part of someone's death no matter what the age. I gathered a great deal of knowledge about labor and delivery and clearly discovered that no matter how much we knew about the process, God was still in control. The hours and days I spent in Labor and Delivery were preparing us for the labor experience of our third child long before his conception. I loved to care for natural laboring patients and help them to accomplish something most people thought was impossible. I also taught childbirth classes for the hospital. I loved this! Working with new moms and helping them to make educated decisions about the life inside of them. As parents, our choices and leadership skills affect so much.

After watching and helping women deliver hundreds of babies naturally, I learned that positioning of the mom and the baby working together could make the journey pleasant or make it pure hell. I was not concerned about the labor with Koby. I had delivered two healthy happy babies in the past without pain medication, and I felt like a professional now. Probably a bit too proud. Pride comes before the fall.

Since our first pregnancy, I have delivered our babies from the first induced contraction in less than four hours. Due to these circumstances, the doctor had decided after Kora's induction we should not try to labor without being at the hospital. All that went well with Kendra and she was born in about 4 hours from the onset of induced contractions as well.

But this was the third child and we lived an hour away from the hospital now, so of course Koby would be induced too. When I arrived at the hospital, the department was full and they didn't have a bed for me. We waited in the waiting room. Finally, the room was ready, but the staff were stressed about having an induction with the department full.

"Another patient to sit on all day!" I heard one of the nurses say.

My doctor heard it too. "Mark my words, she will have the baby in 3 hours," he said.

No pressure on me, but we had the induction agent placed and the contractions began, and so did the diarrhea. It was awful. I think 27 times in the course of three hours. My bottom was raw and I felt constant pain and pressure. No relief from the contractions. I wanted to push.

"You are only 6-7 cm. It is not time yet," the staff said.

Now here was where the logical part came in after 5 years in the labor room. 6-7 cm and stuck. Something was wrong. The third baby and 5 to 10 cm should have gone very quickly and my cervix was making no change. *Oh Lord what now?* It took me a while to write all of this, but the events all happened in a very short amount of time.

We had decided from very early on in our married life I would not take narcotics to deliver babies due to the effects on the moms and babies. However, the pain wouldn't go away and I knew I needed to relax and get some relief. Everyone in the room was shocked when I said I needed an epidural. No matter how I looked at it, it was still narcotics and the baby would receive them. I knew Linda, our nurse and my best friend for years, was willing to do whatever I needed. Kevin couldn't believe I was giving up on one of our dreams, but there was no time to talk about it. I knew I needed to get in the position of getting the epidural more than I needed the medicine. Logic, which was difficult to come by during the transition phase in labor, told me just the curling around the baby was going to help. Koby's heart rate was all over the place, and the contractions would not fully relax so I had no relief between the strong contractions.

"Please check me one more time before the anesthesiologist gets here," I managed to get out.

I was still 6-7 cm, and the baby's heart rate cycled between the 60's and 150's. Not good. *Lord please do something or there will be an emergency cesarean section in the operating room.*

Anesthesia finally arrived at the room and we raised the bed. Kevin stepped to the other side to hold me so I would not move while the needle was placed into the epidural space of my spine.

"Ok," the anesthesiologist said. "The procedure is over. We will give you some medicine now."

"No need to give any medicine," I replied, "I am sitting on the baby!"

"No you aren't, you are only 6-7 cm," the anesthesiologist replied.

Kevin pushed me back in the bed and the baby was lying there for real.

The obstetrician had been waiting outside the door and he ran into the room. No gloves for this delivery.

There was nothing sweeter than the sound of his cry. I just wanted to hold him right then.

"Toni, you have to wait," the doctor said. "The cord is so short, it will have to be cut before he can come to your abdomen."

Wow! All of that revealed at that moment. It was God's plan and not ours; we were just the vessels through which he worked. Koby's cord was less than 11 inches long, hardly long enough to get down the birth canal. The story was completely revealed at that moment. Thank you Lord.

All the crazy heart tones were in response to him trying to get out but not having enough length in the cord to do so. The cervix would not change because there wasn't enough length to the baby's cord for his head to engage completely. And the unbearable pain I felt was so I would get into the only position possible for him to be able to make it out without an abruption of the placenta.

Upon examination of the cord, it was just short, and the fattest cord any of us in the room had ever seen. Still to this day when we sneak a peek at Koby's belly button, it resembles an innie and an outie all at the same time, just to remind all of us of the true power in the Spirit and our miracle natural labor experience. Tons of kisses were shared abundantly that day!

Koby Landon was born on the 4th of November. What a blessing. Kevin was the last of his generation, so it was up to us to have a male child so the name would continue. Kevin of course told me this didn't matter, but he was on the phone with his dad before the cord was cut. This became the most amazing Christmas I ever had spiritually in my life. The Lord was so real and spoke to me so often. When I looked at Koby, I could not help but think every time, *this is how Mary must have felt*. The Christmas lights were awesome, the tree was terrific, the cookies were cool, and the gifts were generous, but the spiritual encounter was most significant. It was a wonderful winter. The girls loved their new brother, and we played and had family time until the snow broke.

Then we began to feel the itch again. Lord, what now? Can't we just have a break? No, there were so many to help.

We met a woman through our church who began to inspire us to look at houses again. What we did not know at the time was that she and her family would be terrific tenants and they would facilitate the process by helping take care of our kids while we worked. They were even willing to help with the renovation process itself. So we called Eric again and asked if he was interested in another house. He needed the data and how we would work the money situation out. We talked about the details, and suggested that they buy the house with their cash and Kevin and I would pay for the cost of the renovations. We could discuss how we would be paid for the labor later. We knew they would recognize our sweat equity since we all valued the relationship and trusted the Lord for the relationship that was being built between the four of us. We kept track of everything and almost dollar for dollar, the cost of materials for the renovations equaled the cost of the house. There was a lot of work to be done again. During this phase, we built some very significant relationships in our lives, not only with Eric, but also with the new tenant to be and her family. It was a joyous time and the home was fabulous when we finished. They were able to move in just in time for the holidays and enjoy a family Christmas in their own place.

# Chapter 15

## Evelyn Doreen (Sparling) Jahn

## September 29, 1929 –August 29, 2009

We took a small break to enjoy the holidays and have some family time. The holidays in our home are special to us. Jesus had delivered us from the curse of eternity in Hell and we all love to celebrate His birthday. We had traditions of our own that the children adored and things we tried to do to bless others.

I loved coffee and kisses, but I also adored cooking and baking for others. This started from a very early age. My grandmother was an awesome cook, and I spent every Saturday as a child with her. They farmed a large amount of acreage in Michigan, and there was always a gathering at breakfast, lunch, and dinner. Grandma and I cooked and cleaned each time I went to visit. She loved to get me to put her hair up in rollers and massage her feet. I remember when I was in second grade grandma fell and broke her leg. I took care of her, rubbed her down with lotion, gave her crazy hairdos, and played in her bathroom cabinets looking for crazy things to make her laugh.

During the time with my grandmother was when I felt the tugging on my heart to become a nurse. I clearly remember her telling me how great I was at taking care of people and I should become a nurse when I got older. Those were the paths that were preparing to take me to a future only God knew about. We made so many memories together. She loved to go to garage sales and talk on the phone. She had the longest phone cord I had ever seen in my life. She had become very proficient at talking and working, so the cord had to be long enough to allow the jobs to be accomplished. She cooked and baked and I loved to eat whatever she made. There are days I wish I could still put a call in to her like I used to do.

"Grandma, I am done with my work at Dad's. Can I come down?"

"Of course, Toni," she always said.

She adored her grandchildren and made sure they all were treated equally, and everyone vouched for that. But in my heart, I knew I was the favorite and the feeling was mutual. Grandma made such an impact on my life as I looked back and reflected on what she did without even knowing it. The three words she lived by were accept, approve, and appreciate. She might not have approved of all my actions, but she approved of me, the person The Lord made me.

The table was always full at grandma's, not just with people but also with food, and I learned how to set a table from her. She performed a salad check, starch check, meat check, vegetable check, and dessert check and everything would be served with coffee and kisses after the milking of the cows was done. She was the one who built the foundation of what family traditions were about from a very early age for me. There was never a doubt about what we were doing for Christmas because going to Grandma's was going to win every time. She wrapped gifts for days and weeks before and loved to shop for everyone. There was always plenty to go around and it was a blast for everyone.

Grandma always had Santa show up with candy and gifts and we thought for sure we could see him fly away in his sleigh. Grandma and I spent hours together as I grew older talking about things that were significant and things I should do and should not do because it was the sort of thing that girls of virtue didn't participate in. Grandma and I would talk about the relationship she shared with Jesus and she was more vocal about this as she aged. She knew He was a significant part of my life, and my will was to please Him with the things I did in my journey.

Sometimes I longed for days that grandma and I could share a coffee and just reminisce, but The Lord took her home far too early in my life. Grandma became very ill and took to bed for about five long years. When I meet God this will be something I will ask Him. Why did some people have a long drawn out departure and others were quickly snatched? No amount of coffee or kisses could help me understand that in this world. That was God's timing and not mine, and I had to accept that He knew what was best for us all. That was a difficult time in my life and as I look back, I knew I might have done things differently if I could do them over, but we don't get to hit rewind in life. We had Kora and Kendra while grandma was in the nursing home and we visited seldom, not because I didn't love grandma, but because the woman I knew was already gone. This disturbed my soul, and often when I visited, it disturbed grandma's as well. Her caretaker would tell me grandma hadn't responded to anyone in days, but when I came with the girls we would have our own conversation and she always knew when I left. We would both cry and this made my heart ache. When grandma passed, dad called me right away. I went to the funeral home to make the arrangements with him, and I knew this would be hard for both of us. We sat with the funeral director, talked about how we needed things to be done, and knew there would be many people there, and would want people to talk if they felt led.

Grandma passed away right around her birthday in September, and I was pregnant with Koby at the time. It was only six weeks until delivery, but I knew I needed to speak at the funeral for the sake of all the grandkids who loved her and for her children who needed to be loved at this time of loss. I selected some verses that I was led to by The Lord and talked about the top 10 things grandma loved, including the number one thing being her grand kids. She just wanted to build into our lives, and I know if she were here now she would see that she did and we could talk about all this over coffee and kisses.

The traditions we have established in our family have nothing to do with anything that the world values or understands. We came up with some things we thought would be fun for our kids and blessing to others, and they have stuck. Bake! We bake for days! This book could have been titled *Coffee, Cookies, and Kisses.*

All six of us baked for three full days. We created cookies, candies, breads, muffins, fudges, and fun. Then we took almost everything we made and created Christmas trays and gave it away to all of those who had blessed us throughout the year. We put a nice family photo and a card on the tray and spent the afternoon and evening delivering 25 to 30 bountiful trays. Some of our tenants joked that they only stayed living in our houses to get their Christmas gift. It made us all feel good and helped our children see that adding value and being a blessing to someone else was the greatest gift in the world. It felt good to make others smile.

Shop. That was what I did. I think I got this from grandma, not because the kids needed a thing, but I loved to see them smile. Shop. That was what they did, for me and for each other, and for someone we knew who was in need. We never adopted a family from any organization; we just went out and found our own. Either one of our tenants was struggling, someone in our church had suffered a setback, or a local family was dealing with the consequences of a hospitalization. We never had trouble finding a family in need.

After the shopping, the wrapping part began. We didn't celebrate Santa Clause in our home. We liked to celebrate the truth, so we chose not to participate with those activities. The kids knew why and didn't mind at all. We would take them to the store and have them pick their own wrapping paper, but it couldn't match anyone else's.

Kevin and I would have a wrapping party after the kids went to bed. We would have some music, lots of paper and tape, and maybe a little wine. We wrapped each child's gifts in their own distinctive paper, that way no nametags were needed and we could accomplish more at a faster pace. Then we divided their gifts into five groupings; most of the time we tried to place their gifts in bags.

Then, on Christmas Eve, we hid the bags with their gifts around the house. The older kids got more difficult hiding places, and the younger ones got the more obvious places.

On Christmas morning, we read from the bible as a family and thanked Jesus for the day. Then the fun would begin. They all went looking for their first bag of presents. We would then gather back around the tree and each one took turns opening their stuff. They were allowed to play with them, try them on, or put them away. After that we would do something together as a family like eat breakfast, sing songs, read a book, have a dance performance, or do anything to be making memories. This would go on for several hours, then the children went looking for the next bag and we repeated the process. The kids adored this, and we would finally finish opening gifts at 9:30 at night.

Our children did not receive more than other children did, we just did it differently to be able to enjoy the entire time together as a family unit. Of course, there was coffee and kisses involved throughout the day, and it was an amazing time. We counted our blessing and thanked God for letting us be a vessel to be used.

# Chapter **16**

## A Time for Expansion

We began our real estate adventure in 2008 with one small house and not knowing where our method would lead us. We always knew we wanted to be financially free and able to invest time into the people's lives around us that we knew, loved, and cared about. I never forgot the old saying: methods are many, principles are few, methods always change, but principles never do.

Real estate was not the method we ever dreamed we would use to bless others and live life abundantly, but God knew it when we were but a sparkle in His eye, and He has never let us down. After that adventure started, we were smart enough to write down where that adventure was going to take us. Our goal was to have financial freedom before we were 50. What would financial freedom allow us? It would allow us to buy back our time, invest into people's lives, and do the things we found important. We considered the following five things to be important: Faith, Family, Friends, Fitness, and Fun.

As the real estate adventure grew, I felt the need to improve our lifestyle. There was nothing wrong with the way we were living, but I saw that if we could take advantage of the real estate market, we could decrease our expenses and get out of the rat race quicker.

We still had our goal of having four children and prayed for that blessing. We quickly became pregnant, but things didn't feel quite right. By that time, I had been working in Maternal Fetal Medicine for a couple years, and every patient I saw was having some kind of complication. Subconsciously, I must have believed everyone had problems with a pregnancy. A few weeks after the positive pregnancy test, I began having back pain and didn't feel well. I decided to call my doctor.

"Are you cramping?" The doctor asked with a bit of concern in his voice.

"I don't think so," I replied. "I think it is just back pain." That was nothing new because I have an old back injury as a result of a car accident when I was 20.

"Well, rest up and call me later. Sooner if anything changes," he said.

The next day I started to have some spotting, but it was Sunday morning and we needed to go to church. As the song, *You Give and Take Away* played during our church service, the tears streamed down my face as I knew I was not going to carry that pregnancy to term. No one else knew why I was crying except Kevin.

We went home and there was more spotting, but it would go away with wiping, and it was more pinkish than red. Maybe I shouldn't be alarmed, I thought. I now believe this was denial since we wanted everything to have the best possible outcome. Kevin went to work on Monday, Valentine's Day, and I called my mom and told her I was pregnant, but was probably going to miscarry and I needed her to come and help me. She came as quickly as she could and we met Kevin at the doctor's office.

I passed the small fetus in the doctor's office, the ultrasound presented an empty uterus, and the exam revealed a closed cervix. The doctor was shocked that it was all over so quickly and the cervix was closed. He gave me some medicine, apologized, and told me to rest for a few days.

"One normal period and you can try again," the doctor said. "That's all I am asking of you."

Ok, we could handle that, but I also told Kevin if we didn't have a baby by the end of the year, I didn't want to have any more kids. I wasn't getting any younger, and I didn't want the children to be too far apart in age. We each mourned differently for the child we would never meet until we passed on to be with our Lord. We were both of the mindset that it was all part of Gods plan.

I was sad and would find myself crying for no reason, and Kevin acted stoic for a couple of days, but then it caught up with him as well. What I regret was that I wasn't there with him when his emotions took over. I wasn't there to hold him and let him know I was feeling the same. I know he wanted to be strong for me, but I needed to see he was hurting too.

A month later, I had a normal period and a few weeks after that I picked up a pregnancy test at the dollar store. I went to work that morning and waited until the end of the day. I took the pregnancy test which was absolutely positive and wheeled out the due date of the 21st of December. Wow, that was cutting it close to the end of the year! I grabbed a card at the store and put the pregnancy test in it and wrote, *Just wanted to give you an early Christmas present.*

I met up with Kevin after work at the house he was working on. He was fixing the toilet or tiling the bathroom, and when he opened the card, he was shocked! We were both elated and he loved my method of delivery. We worked the rest of the spring to finish the house for the new tenants. It was more painting, wallpapering, sanding floors, ripping out junk, replacing and fixing plumbing, hanging new lights, and doing yard work, but we enjoyed every minute of the journey. I felt great and things were going wonderfully.

Now the desires of my heart were beginning to overtake our reality. I wanted more space outside for the children. We had one boy already, and what if the next child was another boy? There was no place here for these kids to ride dirt bikes, fix cars, or grow gardens. So the journey began again to look for a home with some property. We prayed and asked for God's clear guidance in what we should do. We quickly found a home in our price range on ten acres close to the church. The house was not quite what I wanted, but I decided to settle for the house since we loved the property and the barn was fabulous.

The house could be great, but it was just not my style. However, I convinced myself that because everything else was there, we would make it great. I packed our boxes and was determined to put everything away that we would not need until the house was finished. Boxes and paper, tissue and towels wrapped everything, and we clearly marked these boxes so we would know what needed to be put in storage and what we would need to live with.

Once again, we would go to the house and dream about what was going to be. I knew you got what you pictured in your mind! But wait, what if it was not God's plan and you pictured it? How would that turn out? Would you still get what you pictured?

# Chapter 17

## The End of a Dream or a Nightmare?

We were going to have to rent out our old house and live in the new one while we renovated it. I was used to this and it would not have bothered me. Living out of boxes was no big deal and I could handle that, but don't mess with my kids. We finally got all the details worked out, but on the morning before we were to close on the house, the phone rang.

"Where are you? You need to sit down! We cannot close on the house." Ms. T exclaimed.

"What are you talking about? My whole house is packed and we are supposed to begin moving tomorrow."

"I know, but they can't clear the title and the foreclosure was done wrong. They are going to refund your money and that is all there is too it." We will be able to possibly buy it back when it gets all the way back through the legal process"

"How long will that be?"

"Maybe 12-18 months."

"Oh Lord that's too long," I said. "I am leaving my boxes packed. God has a plan, but the window shade is closed right now and I can't see what it is." At this point, I was six months pregnant and thank God, we had not leased the house, so at least we weren't homeless.

We had all the houses wrapped up by that time, and we were going to enjoy the Fall all the way into the Christmas season. We prepped for Christmas as usual and left all the boxes packed. The walls were bare and the closets were empty, but we believed God was going to reveal a far greater plan. It was not too long after the closing fell through that I broke down and sobbed. I confessed to Kevin that I had had a terrible nightmare.

I dreamt that we bought the farm and closed on the property. The home was beautiful and the grounds were immaculately groomed. All that we had envisioned came true in the dream. The kids loved playing in the barn in the hay and feeding the horses and chickens. But one day while they were out playing in the hay mound Kora swung off the top of the bales and accidentally hung herself.

I could not shake that vision from my head. I sobbed as I told Kevin about the dream. I knew the house was what we wanted and we said we would wait for it, but I thought that was God's way of telling us that was not His will and there was something far greater in store.

Kevin and I both agreed, and I could not drive over to the house anymore without seeing Kora's body dangling from the beams in the barn. I would never be able to live there. If we pursued this and something happened to our little girl, I would never forgive myself. The Lord worked in mysterious ways.

# Chapter **18**

## **And Yet Another Miracle**

We prepared for the arrival of our fourth child. Kam Logan was brought into the world with a fabulous birthing experience on the 14th of December, 2011. He was another miracle from above and a perfect addition to the Barnett clan. Once again, we could not have enjoyed the experience nearly as much as we did without the assistance of great people in our lives. Linda and Chantel were both very instrumental in the birthing process and helped us to capture it forever on film. It was beautiful and amazing all at the same time. I will never forget the spiritual closeness that delivery brought between me, my soulmate, and our Lord and Savior.

Have Faith, and when in doubt, continue to Pray and know the Lord's plan is far greater than ours is.

Kam was born on a Wednesday morning, and I believe we went home from the hospital on Friday afternoon. Baby dedication was going to be on Sunday morning at church. We sent Ms. T a message that the baby was born and we would see her on Sunday at church if she would be so kind as to come to the service to enjoy that moment with our family. The Lord had blessed us with a fantastic friend and relationship in her and she would come to our church when we invited her for the kid's stuff, but being raised in the Kingdom hall of the Jehovah's Witnesses, she didn't attend services with us on a regular basis. You see, I was praying for Ms. T from the day I met her. I believed and still do believe The Lord has great plans for her life and she will be abundantly blessed. More times than not, though, it was impossible to convince a non-believer of that. So I continued to pray and let God show up in her life. We shared stories, secrets, and lots of coffee.

Coffee & Kisses

When Kam was born, she was in Aruba on vacation and was not able to visit us in the hospital so the first time she would lay eyes on this baby boy would be at the dedication. Now y'all don't know Ms. T, but she was always late, and late to church on the Sunday before Christmas and baby dedication gets you only one thing - a seat in the front row! From the time she walked in the place and laid eyes on that little humble face, the Holy Spirit went to work. Wow, what a day! I have no idea what happened to her, except she knew she had to surrender her life to The Lord for things to be different, and that she did. Thank you Jesus!

So many events happened in the next few months for both of us. The power of a team when The Lord was in the center was unstoppable. Looking back, I didn't always remember the difficult times, but they were there. The one thing I did remember was The Lord carrying us through when we didn't know what to do.

"That house you wanted just came back on the market," Ms. T told me over the phone a few days after Christmas. "What do you and Kevin want to do about it?"

"Let's put one final offer in on it," I replied. "Before we do, though, I need to tell you about a dream I had. I dreamt that we got the house and Kora accidentally hung herself when she was jumping off the hayloft in the barn. I could never forgive myself if something happened to Kora."

"You know you are never going to get that house," she said. "The Lord has made that clear to you. Don't even bother putting in an offer!"

She was absolutely right! But what neither of us knew was what was coming.

And so we began our search for our new place. Ms. T sent me listings and I looked them over, disposing of the things I didn't even want to look at and marking the others as possibilities.

Of course, in the meantime, we bought two more houses for the business: one to rent and one to fix up and sell. We had a ton of work to do and Ms. T called it Sunny Dump because there was so much work to do. We carted three small children and one newborn with us to work on these places, dirt grime, and all. The girls were amazing helpers with the baby, and they helped with cleaning, painting, and picking up trash. Koby tended to run in and out all day long and slept in the Pack and Play while we worked.

One day while taking a break from painting, I was looking through the listings from Ms. T. There it was! The listing of the house on ten acres in Grand Blanc. Kevin was in the next room painting and I yelled in to him, "Kevin, Here is a house on ten acres for sale. It is listed at $199,999.00." I waited a few seconds to see if he fell off the ladder.

"Toni, no way!" he yelled back at me. "You know we can't afford that. You aren't working and besides we have so much going with these houses."

"I know, Kevin," I replied. "But it doesn't hurt to dream, does it?" Kevin went back to painting in the other room and I finished my break and picked up my paintbrush. I painted for about half an hour until I couldn't take it anymore.

I walked out onto the front porch with my cellphone. "Ms. T? We want to look at the house on the ten acres!"

"You just don't give up, do you, Toni?" she replied with a laugh. "I can meet you there tomorrow about 11 am. Does that work for you?"

"Sure does. I will see you then." Just after saying that, I remembered that Kevin had to work at the hospital the next day. Oh well, it was my dream.

Ms. T was always late, so the kids and I beat her to the property. It was late in January, and Michigan was experiencing what we called a January thaw. It would warm up for a few days just to make a mess with mud and water. That day, it was very muddy out and the snow had covered the property very nicely. The grounds looked amazing. A winding lane lined by blue spruce trees led down to a large pond, a beautiful river cradled the property on two sides, and beautiful trees planted strategically around the property completed the landscape. Besides the house, there was a run in shed, a small little barn, and a large horse barn.

The house sat off to the left of those buildings, and we pulled up and parked in the muddy driveway, waiting on the woman with the key. We were all in awe of the property, and once again, I found myself dreaming of what I could do with this little piece of heaven on earth. I was anxious and nervous. I was dreaming too far out of our price range!

I think I was already picking out paint colors in my head when Ms. T showed up and we went into the house. The inside was unfinished with exposed 2x4 studs. The windows were all new, there were new doors and a new roof on the outside, but inside was pretty much a shell. A big shell, like 6,000 square feet of a shell. Wow!

We had put this in our dream circle years ago, but had no idea how that would ever work for us on a nurse's salary. I stood at the bottom of the stairs and everywhere I looked, I saw possibilities.

"Whoever buys this house would be crazy," I said. "It will take a hundred grand easy to finish it the way it needs to be done."

Ms. T looked over at me and saw the stars in my eyes. Actually, I am sure they were circling around my head.

"And you would just be that crazy one," she said as she shook her head.

We left the house and she closed the door behind me. My thoughts were racing. We couldn't live in the house the way it was, and there was no way we could borrow the money to finish it unless I went to work fulltime. I couldn't possibly do that with four children under the age of seven. Why Lord had you brought this temptation to me? Still, the dream was strong.

"Let's walk around and go look in the horse barn," Ms. T said. She unlocked the door and the world was changed instantly. The horse barn had been renovated and changed into three apartments. Not all of them were finished, but there were six bedrooms and three bathrooms, a kitchen and a laundry room.

"Ms. T, do you think I could rent the apartments and take the extra money to finish the house?" I asked hesitantly.

"I don't see why not, but we will have to call the township."

Of course, the township gave us the entire story on what was going on with the house and the answer was NO! It was zoned single family and the only way to rent those apartments was to go to the zoning board and have it changed to multi family. We were not interested in that at the time. We surely were not confident enough to make presentations to governmental bodies.    We knew that would be a long process and might not work either.

Just because the devil was lurking didn't mean we quit working. Satan would always try to destroy any dream that brought more glory to God, but sometimes I had to have enough faith to remember that we belonged to God.

Lord there has to be a way, I thought while I stood in the Township office. "Ok," I asked the clerk, "can we live in the barn while we work on the house?"

"We will have to do an inspection and you will need to bring some things up to code since no permits were pulled when the renovations were done. But otherwise that will not be a problem."

We drank gallons of coffee and prayed our little hearts out. Lord, if this was supposed to be, please let it work. We submitted a bid for only $90,000.00 since the house needed so much work, and we guessed the bank knew the right person would have to come along. However, the bank rejected our offer.

I called my parents and told them about the house. "Mom, if you and dad would submit a bid also, it will force the bank to look at two offers at the same time, and they may be more willing to accept ours. Kevin and I are planning to offer $135,000.

"Of course, Toni," mom replied, "but you know we don't want a project of that size. Our bid will be way lower than yours."

"Thanks, mom." They submitted their bid that afternoon, and a few days later we found out that the bank had accepted our bid.

Now for the financing. You see we no longer qualified for regular financing because we had so many properties. I called our commercial lender and let them know what I needed to do. That sounded great, but they required 30% in cash as a down payment. I had forgotten about that. You guessed it - we were almost flat broke since we had just bought two houses for cash.

Like I had said before, just because the devil was lurking didn't mean we quit working. If we felt in our heart that it would be a blessing to others, and it was the right thing to do, we looked for ways to make it work. I called Eric in Texas and told him what we needed to have.

"Of course I'll help you," he said. "That sounds like a great property. I can only loan you about half of the down payment, though, as we have a project of our own down here."

I think I thanked him a hundred times. We would have the money from Eric in a couple of days. I talked to our lender again, and I found we could take just about $15,000 equity out of one of the houses we just bought to secure the rest of the cash we would need for the down payment. We were all set. Devil be gone!

Where did people like Eric and Andrea come from? Who would loan friends that kind of money? How did they get in our lives?

None of it made sense when my human mind tried to figure it out, but when I trusted that it was all part of God's plan, it made perfect sense.

So in 2012, we bought three houses in six weeks and had to arrange to move, get a renter for the home we were living in, and try to complete the work on the houses for the business. I thought the Saint the Lord had put in my life was going to kill me. I had all the ideas, but he made them come true. Kevin never complained, he just put his bib overalls on and went to work. Frank Betcher, in his book *How I Raised Myself from Failure to Success in Selling,* said success often showed up as a pair of bib overalls and was a lot of work. And boy was it ever!

# Chapter 19

## What are You Going To? Not What You are Going Thru!

In February on a bright bitter cold day while we were working in Sunny Dump, a gentleman came to the house and asked if there was any work he could do to help us out. Normally, we liked to do things ourselves, but we had so much work to do, and I despised plaster work and sanding drywall.

"Do you know how to finish drywall?" I asked hopefully.

"Let me go get Elder. I will be right back," he replied.

A few minutes later, in walked a 77 year-old man with a gray beard down to his belly He could have been Mosses himself! He explained that they were looking for extra work because it was difficult to live off their retirement incomes alone. He calculated how much time he thought it would take to finish the drywall and gave us a price.

Kevin and I looked at the price and then at each other. "Can you start tomorrow?" we asked in unison.

I believed there was a direct connection between God hearing what's in your heart and supplying your needs. You just needed to trust and believe. God knew I had not intended to finish the drywall and would be hiring someone to come and do that job. He also knew Kevin and I needed Elder Ken and Willie in our lives for far greater reasons than finishing drywall. Remember earlier in the book when I talked about Kevin needing a mentor in his life? God brought them to our door through this crazy business we were trying to bless others with.

Elder said early on , "I am 75% spiritual and only 25% physical, so what The Lord chooses to do with me now I am content with."

"That is amazing, Elder," I said. I hope I can get to that point in my life someday." I meant every word of that.

That old man has prayed for us and over us as if we were his own children. He has brought me to tears more than once and he knew The Lord was going to continue to bless us beyond measure.

"Elder," I said one afternoon shortly after meeting him. "I would like you to pray for Ms. T. She is the most wonderful person, and wants more than anything to be married, but she never seems to find the right guy."

Without even pausing to think about it, Elder said, "Tell Ms. T to be faithful to The Lord, and he will bring the right person."

I shared the story with Ms. T, and we both laughed about it since all the guys she had dated had no potential. But July came and so did a man named John. John became a born again believer at 17, and he was just what she needed to guide her in the spiritual leadership the relationship would require to grow and prosper. They were engaged in September and married in December. Lots of coffee and kisses.

Back to the house and ten acres on Belsay Road. We moved into the renovated barn in the beginning of May. The Lord brought us a renter for our previous home, and we tried to settle in to the apartment lifestyle – in a barn! This was a big struggle for me. We had four children and there was really no place to put things away. Sure, there was a playroom, and the all had a bedroom, but the closets did not have doors because the previous owner had taken them. The rooms were small and the bathrooms were tiny. There were no places to put linens, and the kitchen was so small that I couldn't have the refrigerator and the dishwasher open at the same time. I had to limit the amount of groceries I bought because I only had seven small cabinets for food storage. Were we Blessed? Beyond measure! It was not about what we were going through; it was about what we were going to.

Dream, Struggle, Victory.

There was a lesson to be learned here right? Yes there was. The lesson was that it was not about stuff. Stuff could clutter and choke my life. We needed to keep the main thing the main thing. We would Bless others and all those things would be added on.

I did not know Kevin was struggling with the Belsay Road purchase. He loved the home and adored the property, but he had prayed every day since we bought it that The Lord would not allow it to be our financial ruin.

I had no idea about Kevin's feelings until shortly after I received a phone call in August.

"Hi, my name is Jeri," the caller said. "I was referred to you by a friend of yours. I am interested in hiring you for a job for the next 18 months."

Jeri spent the next five minutes describing the job to me and letting me know about the compensation.

"Thank you, Jeri," I said, "but I am not interested. I have small children, I own a business, and I don't have time for a job." I hung up the phone.

"Who was that?" Kevin asked with heightened interest.

"It was a recruiter by the name of Jeri She wants me to come to work for the next 18 months. I told her I was too busy with the business and the kids."

"What did she offer you?" Kevin asked as he tried to control his excitement.

I told him the hourly rate.

Elder Ken was standing there and did the quick math. "WOW girl! Who gets a call out of the blue with an offer like that? Someone who is blessed and highly favored by The Lord Almighty!"

Kevin looked at me and said, "I think you better call her back. That would mean we could finish the entire house with just the money you could earn from that one job. I have been praying this house wouldn't ruin us financially."

I called Jeri back. She told me she would let me know when the ink on the contract was dry. However, the ink never came. The company she was working for didn't get the contract, so they had no job to offer me. We were extremely disappointed, but we knew we should pray to let God take care of it.

A few weeks later, Jeri called again. "Would you be interested in trying some travel consulting?" You would have two weeks in Delaware paid for, you would have the weekends off, and Kevin and the kids could travel along as well."

"Absolutely," I said. Who gets blessed so much in life? We had just come to the place in our lives where we were able to bless others, and we were in returned blessed. We spent many hours counting our blessings over a cup of coffee and giving the Glory to The Lord.

After the first trip to Delaware, our lives were changed forever. A huge thank you to Jeri for having enough trust and faith in me that I could be a traveling consultant. The company we worked for began to book trips for us, and we viewed them as mini vacations. We began to work implementing electronic health records. We took the kiddos along and were able to see more of the incredible world The Lord blessed us with. We have met so many people and learned so many things from taking time to sit down and listen to other people's journeys.

Dream, struggle, victory. And of course lots of coffee.

# Chapter 20

## What does Victory Look Like?

Everyone has a different idea of what victory looks like. Mine was different from those of my girlfriends, different from my coworkers, and even different from those of my husband. The important thing about your personal victory is that you know what it is. You need to define it as clearly as you can. Write it down, dream about it, go touch and feel it. If it is a distant destination, clip pictures and put them up on the ceiling in your room so after your nightly prayers you have to stare at them. Get the vision into your soul so it moves and stirs you. When the pain of change is less than the pain to remain the same, you will change.

For example, I have read countless stories about husbands who would change nothing in their relationships until they were served divorce papers. Then they would have to tell their sweet innocent children they were moving out. When a man was stirred emotionally, and the pain was so great it hurt less to change something than it hurts to keep things as they were, then he would make a change, but not until then. It was sad that it often gets to that point. Sometimes that was the point of no return, and once again, Satan had snatched another family.

The one thing I had to learn was to visualize where I wanted to be, not where I was. Victory in my life was not where I was; otherwise, I would already have that victory. I wasn't debt-free yet because I had not become the person who knew how to be debt free. I needed different information from someone else. I had gotten myself to where I was, and if I wanted some things to change, I was going to have to be the one to change some things – with some outside help. Mentors were awesome to help with that.

The next year moved very quickly for us and we had so many blessings. We bought four homes within six weeks. Financially, I felt like things were crazy. All the money seemed to be going out, and there was little return. All we knew to do was to continue to do the work, pay it forward, and believe the Blessing would come back.

The lesson I had to keep reminding myself of was to pray to The Lord without ceasing. I found I prayed more when the bank account was empty because I had to depend on God to take care of our family because we had no other way of doing it and paying all the bills. When the money started to come in, I would lose my focus and become less dependent on The Lord.

The crazy cycle kept continuing, and I learned God had never gone anywhere. I was the one who separated myself from Him and He was just waiting for me to come back. God desires to have a close personal relationship with each and every believer, but we have to desire to move in His direction. When I realized that God, and not money was going to take care of us, I began praying just as hard to The Lord when the bank account had money as I did when it didn't. It seemed weird at first, but sometimes the lesson continued until the lesson was learned. I needed to learn to keep God the focus.

My life could seem a little crazy to everyone else around me, and honestly, I have to say I lived with one big saint and four little ones. They knew me better than the rest of the world, and we were all over the place all the time. We called it LIFE, but I know you have your own life. What I really want to impress upon you is that no matter how busy I got or how crazy it felt, if I lost the focus on the Kingdom and the time I needed with my Creator, nothing else mattered. Do all things for the glory of the kingdom of God.

# Chapter 21

## Unbelievable Baby!

So what did the next chapter of our life look like? UNBELIEVABLE BABY! I really have no other way to explain it. We began consulting, and enjoyed the time we were allowed to invest into other people's lives. That's the only reason you are reading this book. We shared our stories across America with anyone who wanted to listen. Many times people would say WOW, you should write a book and do motivational speaking. We were pure living truth that motivational speaking works. I speak and Kevin gets motivated. Ha Ha.

Our lives started out very different and our level of motivation was still very different, but we came to appreciate that about each other. I will occasionally ask Kevin, "How do you think your life would be if you didn't marry me?"

He always gives a one-word answer, "Boring."

I think he secretly prayed for those days, and sometimes I thought I would just like to surprise him again with a new idea, but he was no longer amused, he just worked hard to help implement the things God brought into our lives.

We found that opportunities were all around, but many times, other people didn't take the time to look for them or seek them out. "They were just lucky," they would say or "Of course it would work for them, he's smart and she is pretty. They had to have money to start."

That was just not the case for us. Ok, maybe he was smart and I was pretty, but we had to learn very essential principles in life and applied them repeatedly and over again to get results.

The life of consulting opened so many new doors for us. Monetarily, it was a huge blessing so we could share with others and stack some money away to finish our beautiful home that we intended to share with others. We both loved to entertain. I loved baking and cooking for a crowd, and for some reason when I say I am cooking the crowd always shows up.

We learned that trusting The Lord with money, whether a little or a lot, was a timeless principle. We had many times in our life when there was no money, and times when there was plenty of money. Life was a lot more fun when there was plenty because we could bless others without worrying about feeding our children.

So we were the new kids on the block of consulting. Kevin continued to work his nursing job to pay our household expenses, and we put money away and blessed others. We went on consulting jobs when we were asked and did our best job - we really tried to let our light shine! We traveled to Tennessee, Delaware, New Jersey, Colorado, Virginia, Texas, Alaska, California, New Mexico, New York, Pennsylvania, West Virginia, Alabama, Arkansas, Louisiana, Illinois, Kentucky, South Carolina, North Carolina, and a few states I probably missed.

When we were asked to take the job, it sounded unbelievable. So unbelievable that we decided to ask the kids what they thought. The girls were nine and seven at the time, and the boys were too young to even know what it meant. I will never forget Kora's response.

"Mom, the Bible says to go into all the world and preach the Gospel," she said with a smile. "We will kind of be like missionaries."

She could not have said the more perfect thing to me at that time. They were not little saints by any means, but we were talking about putting four kids into a van and traveling for a year across the country with nothing more than we could pack. They would have to give up seeing their friends, going to dance class, participating in church or community activities, or even sleeping in their own beds.

People asked, "What are you thinking, or are you? That will be too hard on the kids. Do you know what you are doing? Who is going to help you when you are both working?"

We heard it all, but when the DREAM was big enough, the facts didn't count.

Remember the principle of writing down what you want? Long ago, we had put in our dream circle that we wanted to travel and home school our children. Don't be shy about what you dream, because you can't dream bigger than God can, so you need to dream as big as you can. All of this was our dream, and we were going to get paid for it!

Who got to live like that? We were so blessed and have been so appreciative of it all. Once all of the travel got rolling, Kevin was going to have to resign from his nursing job. I wasn't sure how he felt about that. We would have no benefits with the new jobs, and we would have to always trust The Lord to take care of our bills. What a step for me! Kevin couldn't wait, but I was the one who wasn't sure. Kevin had worked there for 15 years, but he could not wait to leave. His coworkers gave him a party, and cried tears of joy. There was sadness, as they knew in their hearts that once he left, he wouldn't come back.

Our family went out on the road together. We had long hours of working and shared fun family times exploring the local areas for things to do with the kids. It was very interesting to see how unique and how similar we really were no matter where we went. Certain parts of the country were much more welcoming and receiving, certain parts were more open about their faith, and certain parts were more focused on doing as little as possible with the greatest return. We learned we really didn't need anything except the clothes on our backs, but certainly, coffee and kisses were a fabulous addition to all the other blessings.

In the last year, there have been too many God Moments to mention, but I felt the need to include the following one because of the lesson it teaches. We were in Texas in March for a consulting job. Our company called and asked if I could go to Nashville for the weekend to do some training. Of course, I could - that was what I did. I flew around, met people, and helped them with their needs.

I got on the flight feeling very excited since I knew I would be meeting my girlfriend who was working there for the same company. We finished the day of training, and headed to Outback Steakhouse for dinner. As I bit into my mushroom appetizer, I checked the messages on my phone and saw that Kevin had called. I put the phone on speaker and hit play.

"Hi Toni. There is freezing rain here and I am about frozen. Kendra fell on the steps and her puppy got away. We have been out looking for the dog for an hour and cannot find her anywhere. Please call when you get this. Love you."

I put down my fork and called him back immediately. "Kevin, is Kendra Ok? Where did the dog go? Why does it always have to be her pet?" I knew I sounded sharp and was pounding him with questions, but I was tired from a long day of working.

"I don't know," he replied with teeth chattering, "but I am freezing and I can't look any longer."

"OK, dear," I said as I softened my tone. "Can you get the girls on the phone?" A few seconds later, Kora was on the line. "Kora, I want you to put your coat on and go knock on the neighbors' doors." At that time, we were living in a gated apartment community, and I thought someone probably had picked the dog up and taken her inside since it was freezing and raining out.

Coffee & Kisses

Kora and Kendra went out knocking on doors while I stayed on the phone with them so they weren't nervous.

"No one has seen the dog, Mom," Kora finally said dejectedly.

"Keep the faith, Kora," I said as I was feeling mine slipping away. "Go ask Katelyn your babysitter to help you look for the puppy."

"Ok, mom," she said with as much optimism as she could muster.

"Call me in a little while," I said. I felt so terrible not being there to help them.

I immediately started calling and texting everyone I knew from Michigan to Florida to Texas to Arkansas to pray for this little puppy. That was a worldwide prayer to watch over that dog and bring her home. What else could I do from so far away? I was in Nashville, and they were in Texas. I called the apartment manager.

"Emmi, Kendra fell down the stairs and her puppy got away. When you get in tomorrow morning, can you ask around to see if someone found the puppy?"

"I will call security now," she replied. "I am on my way to help them look for the dog."

I burst out crying! Who did that? We only met her a month earlier when we moved in, and she didn't know us from Adam. It was a Sunday night about 9:30 pm and she was going to help my kiddos look for their doggie. The angels The Lord sent while I couldn't be there. I called the girls back.

"We can't find the dog anywhere! Mom, we are exhausted and freezing!"

"I understand, I think someone already took her in and will take her to Emmie in the morning. Go to bed and pray and The Lord will take care of everything."

"You pray too, OK Mommy?"

74

"Of course I will," I said. I went back to my room still upset that I was not there to hold my little Kendra in her time of distress. I was doing some work on the computer when the phone rang.

"It's Emmie! I found her!"

It was 10:30 pm and she just gotten to the apartment complex. When she drove in, her headlights shone under a maroon Ford truck and she saw something move. She jumped out of her car and discovered that the dog's leash had gotten caught under the tire and the puppy was stuck there. She rescued the dog and took her upstairs. No one could believe she came all the way to help in this time of need.

When I first called Emmie, I was only calling to ask her to have security be on the lookout for the puppy. Emmie lived over an hour from the complex and it was her day off. She did not need to drive all that way or even be concerned about my little ones, but she knew the right thing to do - not because it was the easy thing, but because it was the right thing. The lesson? HELP when called upon, even if you don't know what the result will be. You just might make a little girl and her mother very happy.

Emmie called me back after she returned the puppy and I thanked her countless times. "Emmie you didn't need to do that," I kept telling her.

"Yes I did! The puppy would have frozen to death being out there all night or someone would have run over her. Toni, the Lord led me right to the dog. I know it. I believe it!"

Why did she have to be the one to find her? She got the great reward for being the servant leader. She found the puppy and delivered her back to her overjoyed owners. The next day we showered Emmi with flowers and gift cards to show our appreciation. As I looked back on the event, I knew The Lord was watching over the dog the entire time, but Emmi needed to show up and do her part for His light to shine. Sometimes, 90% of the battle was to show up. We thanked Emmie again and again in our prayers.

The Lord put us here to care for people and to share for people. That was the only way God had to figure out if He could trust us. We needed to care for people expecting nothing in return, and share what we had with people expecting nothing in return. These were two of the things Kevin and I had implemented since the beginning of our marriage. I knew this was why most of the things that happened to us made no sense to the outside world.

People said we were lucky. We preferred the term *Blessed*. We lived by the motto: Labor Under Correct Knowledge and Apply the Knowledge. If we did, then off-the-wall great things happened and we gave the Glory away so God could trust us and do it again. We have had so many God events in our lives; I have only been able to discuss a few of them. We have continued to Praise God with our lives over coffee and kisses. When you showed up at our place, you never knew if you were going to receive the coffee or the kisses, but quite possibly both!

# Chapter 22

## Summing It All Up

I was once again in a hotel room. I needed to finish the book, and I was concerned about the amount of time I was taking out of my life to write it. I had four young children, a real estate business, good friends, a business owner I was mentoring, a commercial building we were closing on, a music publishing company in Nashville, and, and, and... When the job offer came along to *travel in on Monday by noon, and travel out on Thursday by 3 PM*, I wasn't sure I should take it.

"How else are you going to finish *Coffee and Kisses*?" Kevin asked when I told him about the job. "You only get time to write when you are on the road!"

So there I was at the computer in my hotel room. I was only two weeks into a nine-week contract, and my real reason for taking the job was to finish my book! Even with such subterfuge in my heart, I prayed I could be a blessing to those around me and shine His light into this dark world. It got lonely when I was on the road all the time, but it was great growth time. I rarely if ever turned on the TV.

We have not had TV in our home for about 12 years. We got rid of it to get things done. Instead of wasting our time, we wanted to invest our time creating the future we wanted for our children. We invested time into the lives of our children and those around us. I believe the TV is one of Western society's greatest downfalls. As if the time wasted sitting in front of the TV wasn't bad enough, the negative energy it spewed out was even worse. The thing we called entertainment had desensitized us to the point where we as a society were no longer moved emotionally by anything.

In the real world, people got shot, stabbed, committed suicide, and beat their children and spouses. Yet we tolerated that because for years the TV had desensitized us. People fantasized about making their lives like those of the celebrities, but knew in their hearts that those celebrities had not found true happiness either. We wanted our spouses to be like Prince Charming all the time because that was the way it was on TV, right?

A bit farfetched? Hitler wouldn't think so. He began brainwashing his army at the early age of five. His followers schooled the children into believing in his mission and his vision of a superior race and conquering the world. Looking back, it seemed ludicrous that he was able to do that, but when you changed the mold and formed the mind of a child by building their trust and desensitizing them to things, chances were in 20 years you could get them to do whatever you wanted them to do.

It was no wonder that divorce rates were at a record high. Americans had invited Satan's sandbox, the TV, into their homes. They played in it during breakfast, lunch, and dinner. They couldn't even get away from it to pump their gas.

People needed to think. They needed to sit down, have a cup of coffee, and actually have a conversation about an idea. They didn't need to gossip about someone, relive the weekend, dream about a vacation, or catastrophize about current events. Only discussing an actual idea would move their lives forward. More coffee and kisses would be needed – such a transformation could take a long time.

# Chapter 23

## Measuring Success

How did one measure success? I got a small taste of success over the weekend. On Friday, we were all working at one of the houses we were fixing up as a new rental. I was painting, and Kevin was installing flooring. The children had brought one of the barn kittens along, and it was being a bit mischievous.

"The kitten just went down in the crawlspace," Kendra yelled. "Where is the flashlight? We need to find her!"

I put my paintbrush down, found the flashlight, and gave it to Kendra. The two girls went down into the crawlspace.

"We can't find her," they yelled from down in the crawlspace.

I think Kevin was looking for a break from laying the flooring, so he went down also, but he could not locate her either. I didn't care if we found her, so I told the kids not to worry about it. A few minutes later, Kevin went into the bathroom and heard the kitten meowing. He reached down behind the shower and pulled her out. The kids came rushing in, and we sighed in relief that we weren't going to have to have a pet funeral.

I asked the kids not to let the cat out of their sight again. So they played with her, cuddled her, and took her out to the garage to play. It was Halloween day in Michigan, which meant it was snowing, raining, and below freezing. I noticed the girls going in and out of the garage for what seemed like hours.

Kora finally came in with her head down and shuffled her feet a bit before she asked, "Can we go for a walk down the side road a little ways to look for the kitten?"

"Did she get out?" I asked, knowing the answer before I asked the question. I was tired and impatient, but I tried not to sound angry.

"Yes, and we can't find her anywhere. " Kora was overcome with sadness.

Freezing rain was falling, but they were determined to find their small kitten. They returned after about 15 minutes empty handed.

"No luck?" I asked as I stared at their sad faces. "Why don't you go check in the garage again? Maybe she never left."

They exited, then about 10 mins later, they came running in.

"Mom! We found her. We went to the garage like you said and we prayed together and began to look and then we found her! God always answers prayers"

The first thought that went through my head was mission accomplished. They believed in their hearts that God was that real! They believed that when you prayed for something, He listened, and then He answered.

To have the faith of a child. When did we stop believing like that? Maybe the bigger question is, when do we start believing like that? If the family was being eaten alive by Satan, and churches were having a challenging time preaching the Gospel, how could believers grow to know that God wants to be so real in our lives? There was not a chance in Hell, which was right where Satan wanted us to be.

In case you never finish this book, read the last chapter of the only Book that matters. God will triumph over Satan, but there will be a terrible battle. It won't be physical, but it will be warfare, and there will be heartache and despair. The Book tells us the battle for our souls is going on right now in our lives, but Jesus Christ can help us to overcome Satan and win the Kingdom of God for ourselves. We need to surround ourselves with positive influences, be the positive influence, care, and share for others, and read, struggle and grow. Man, there are so many things to do to be a servant leader. More coffee and kisses please.

# Chapter 24

## What's Next?

That last chapter was tough stuff, but I wrote what God put in my heart, and I wrote this book to bring light to the Kingdom that he has allowed us to help Him build. We were only the vessels pouring our lives into others so He could fill us again.

It was the middle of June and the sun was shining brightly in Nashville, TN. I was there on business, and I got a phone call from Ms. T.

"Toni," she said through her tears. "I know you have a special relationship with God. That is why I am calling to tell you that a friend of mine has a prayer request. Her three year-old grandson was in a mowing accident and needs prayers. The child has lost his leg and possibly his arm, and they are not sure how things are going with his brain."

Suddenly the sunshine was gone. I burst into tears and gathered my friends around me and we began to pray for that family and their little boy Truett. I had never met the family and I didn't know the grandparents – they were just friends of a friend. I was so emotionally moved, I couldn't believe it. I cried and cried for the family. I read the website and I shared it with my friend Amy, one of my very best spiritual sisters. We were both so moved by Truett. His story and situation jolted us both spiritually and emotionally. I got the kids and Kevin in the adventure of praying for someone we didn't know and we enjoyed watching God show up. We tracked Truett's progress daily on Caring Bridge to see what the updates were. We saw him progress from being on life support to being extubated, and then going through surgery after surgery. We saw when the rescue team came to visit him in the hospital, heard his first words, saw his smiles, and watched him laughing and playing with his siblings. We got to watch by God's great grace that family be incredible witnesses to their faith in The Lord. We got to watch videos of Truett taking his first steps and learning to run and ride scooters. We were truly amazed at God's healing power and continued to pray for Truett and his family.

I was not sure if I ever had something affect me so much when it had nothing to do with anyone I knew. I have since learned this was God's way of drawing me closer to Him again. I was traveling so much that summer, and I was most often alone. Truett gave me someone to focus on besides myself. I kept thinking *if this was my family how would I react and what kind of witnesses would we be?*

I praised and thanked The Lord often that we had been spared any accidents of that kind so far. I was still thanking The Lord. It all tied together for me when I watched Caring Bridge and saw Truett speak his first words on video.

"Oh, SNAP," he said with a shining face.

Amy, Kevin and I had been working for CHS for about 9 months, and were very quickly realizing that that type of consulting work was soon going to end. We all began talking about other businesses we should start and ways we should make money. We felt since Truett had made such an impression in our lives we should utilize "Oh, SNAP" in our adventures together.

So of course, I was in what I called the looking zone again. I was wondering what to do, and trying to think how we could make all of it work now that the jobs were ending. I found comfort in the phrase, *Be still and know I Am God.*

I just got on the elevator in one of the hotels and the door closed. There was a picture on the door surface of two small children playing with a bushel of snap peas and the words written across the door said - you guessed it - "OH, SNAP!"

I could hardly believe it! Did I really need the words spelled out in front of me to know that it was from God? I already could feel that, but now for sure it had been confirmed. I took a picture and sent it to Amy. We were both in awe of God being so real in our lives.

The very next day, I was driving west on Interstate 74 in Galesburg, Illinois when I saw three large billboard signs in a row. All three were black with white letters. The first one displayed, "Here's your sign." The next billboard displayed, "Dream Big." The final sign displayed, "At the end of your Life, you will meet God." I drove on and thanked the Lord for actually giving me a billboard sign to let me know that He had it all under control. The message was clear, *Dream big, and realize the decisions you make today influence many around you. Dream big and share those dreams with your loved ones over coffee and kisses.*

The conclusion of everything I have written is to share and care about people. We feel we have been extremely blessed in our lives beyond measure. However, with every success there are some key principles that anyone can apply to their own lives. Verses in the Bible are timeless principles.

*"All things are possible through Jesus Christ who strengthens me."*

*"For God so loved the world He gave His only Son that whoever believes in Him shall not parish but have everlasting life. "*

*"Lean not on your own understanding."*

*"The man who does not work should not eat."*

We both accepted Jesus Christ as our Lord and Savior to glorify the Lord's kingdom. This doesn't mean we don't have problems, concerns, challenges, doubts, or are perfect by any means. It only means we have a Lord and Savior who Accepts us right where we are, and have the Bible to guide and direct our paths and decisions. We also have spiritual guides and mentors in our lives who have been hand-selected to have influence on us. We have purposefully allowed books, sermons, people, songs, and experiences to motivate and mentor us.

Kevin and I may not always agree on everything, but we are always on the same team. We often ask ourselves, what is our overall goal? What are we trying to accomplish, and whom are we trying to influence and glorify? Sometimes this gets lost in the heat of the physical work and the depth of the spiritual battle, but if we begin with the end in mind, every time we can wade through the toughest things set out before us.

# Chapter 25

## Three Timeless Principles for Your Journey

When Kevin and I started out, we didn't have any formal tools to work with – we just had our love for each other and our faith in God. Many of you reading this book have that same love and faith, and can easily do what we did and more. As a bit of a jumpstart, though, I would like to discuss some principles that we found to be useful to keep us ever moving toward our goals.

## Principle 1 - The Productive Loop

The Productive Loop is a six-step process we have learned to implement in our lives on a regular basis. It can and will work for you.

### Step 1 – Set Goals

If we never set any goals, we will never hit any goals. The goals can be small or bodacious, just remember that you will need to put in effort in proportion to the size of the goal in order to reach the goal. If this is a new concept to you, you may want to start out small and see how the Productive Loop works for you. What is the best way to eat an elephant? One bite at a time.

Maybe your goal is to exercise, but you have never exercised in your life. To set a goal of running a marathon next week would be unrealistic, but a goal of going to the gym four times this month, eight times next month, and twelve times the following month makes it much more achievable and still shows progress. Setting the goal to be debt-free is awesome! To be debt-free in six months when you have very little extra cash, and $25,000 in credit card debt, is a bit of a stretch as well. However, setting a goal to add an extra $50 payment per month to decrease the balance on the bill is probably very achievable the first month, and maybe $60 the second month, $65 the third month and so on. It takes time, work, and dedication to make changes in our lives. Be willing to give up some things in the short term that others won't, so some day you can have what others can't. Be willing to Give Up to Go Up. Most of all, enjoy the journey.

## Step 2 – Make an Action Plan

It is best to sit down and write the goal out along with the plan of how you are going to get there. We like to attach a reward to ours as well. We involve our children in the process too. Let's say the goal is to finish the repairs on the home we are renovating by a specific date. When we reach the goal, we reward ourselves with a family outing to the waterpark. The kids also know it is important for them to help with the tasks in order to receive the reward. If they don't work, they don't play. They all know how to pick up trash and take it to the dumpster, sweep floors, paint walls, help with the demo of the project, lay tile and hardwood flooring with their daddy, help with installing switch plate covers, vacuum, and wipe down windows. They are learning the principles of working hard to be able to bless others around them.

## Step 3 – Implement the Plan

This part is where the real work comes in. Whatever the goal is there is work to be done to reach it. The work can sometimes be physical, mental, emotional, spiritual, but most often is a combination of all of them. Growing pains occur here. You may be feeling like you are failing here and doing more work than anyone else around you does. That's okay since someday you will be able to celebrate unlike anyone else around you. Don't get sucked in by rumors, hearsay, and popular opinions. Those people are not paying your bills and at the end of the day, you are responsible for you. Stick in there, when the going gets tough, keep going. If you need to take a step backwards to go forward two, it's ok. We are just looking for progress and sometimes the best things mean we have to GIVE UP to GO UP.

## Step 4 – Check the Progress on the Plan

When you set your goals, make sure you associate a time line with them. Remember the time line is to direct you so you know how hard you need to work the plan. It is also recommended that you set a timeline on when to check your progress. If you say you want to lose 30 pounds in six weeks, but never check the progress along the way and the six weeks arrives the scales may give a big surprise, or not. However, the way to ensure you meet the goal is to check your progress along the way. Depending on the size of the goal depends on how often progress should be monitored, every day? Maybe...every week? For sure, every month, may be pushing it to the limits depending on how far out the goal is. Remember, the more you focus on the goal and the progress the easier it is to reach it. We all want you to succeed in whatever measure that is for you. Remember often times the longer we stretch out the timeline the lazier we can be.

## Step 5 – Make Adjustments as Necessary

Once you check your progress, look back at what the original goal was. How far did you come, did you back slide? Why? What distractions were in your way? Were they excuses? How can you overcome them in the future? Who can help you with this? Do you need to re set the goal? Do you need to work the plan harder? Did you look for a mentor who has done this before to give you some tips to success? Do you talk about the goal frequently? Do you envision yourself succeeding?

Answer these questions honestly and adjust the plan again if you need to. Write down the answer to these questions if you are not where you want to be on the timeline. Decide if you need to raise the bar on yourself or move things out of the way that are hindering you form achieving you DREAMS.

What happens when we don't hit the goal? We adjust! So we didn't quite get finished by October, okay can we be done by the middle of November? We dig our heels in and maybe put in a few extra hours, get up early or stay late, and allow no excuses. The goal is in sight and we try to keep our eyes on the prize. Imagine what it feels like to run a marathon when you have never exercised in your life. Imagine what it feels like to be debt-free and have no bill collectors calling every day. Imagine what it feels like to step outside the box and do something that other people only dream of doing. Imagine being able to leave behind your legacy to pass down to the next generations knowing that in the end we will all meet God. Will He say, "Well Done thy good and faithful servant?"

### Step 6 – Repeat the Process

The previous five steps can be used to achieve any goal, but frequently we find that new goals arise once others are achieved. You will find the process exhilarating once you start to achieve your goals, and you will want to set goals that are ever higher. Remember – YOU CAN'T DREAM HIGHER THAN GOD CAN!

## Principle 2 –The Dream, Struggle, Victory, Repeat Loop.

### Step 1 - Dream

DREAM about what you want your life to look like. Go out touch feel and smell it. Test drive cars you can't afford, walk through model homes that you would love to share with someone someday, look at pictures of vacations you want to take, visit shelters where you would love to make a difference, check into charities that need your help and/or money. Do the things to push yourself to get uncomfortable. Then write down the DREAM of what you want your life to look like in the next 5 years, tape pictures of it to your wall. Look at it every day and use it to motivate yourself to be more disciplined with your money. Keep a log of what you spend every day for a month. Write it down and look at the end of the month as to what you CAN GIVE UP so you CAN GO UP. Coffee? (Not for me). Fast food? Eating out?

Smoking? Drinking? Cable TV? Just some ideas of things we were willing to sacrifice in order to pay off debt and put money away to save to invest in real estate.

## Step 2 - Struggle

STRUGGLEs will be there for everyone. The important thing is how we deal with them. Do we control them, or do they control us? Attitude isn't everything; it is the only thing. Do you turn the light on when you walk in the room or turn the light off? Are you the influencer or always being influenced? Stand up when it is not easy. Do the right thing, not because it feels good, but because it is the right thing to do. Care and share your experiences with others so you can help your fellow man. Your experience can help save someone from destroying his or her life. Remember what it feels like to care for someone expecting nothing in return. Sometimes we have to count our blessings as non-material things. Pray as hard as you can and as often as you can. The struggle is real and it takes a lot of work to get out of the Valley. Remember it took David five smooth stones, and a lot of God given Courage to slay the giant in the Valley. David didn't fight from the mountaintop; he was in the Valley, but he didn't give up until he reached his goal and defeated Goliath.

The Struggle will be hard work, but momma said THERE WOULD BE DAYS LIKE THIS. Don't quit! Do what you tell your kids to do. We don't accept it from our kids, so why do we accept it from ourselves? Practice SELF-PARENTING. Discipline yourself and correct the course as you go. Ask questions and plan to do better than you did yesterday. We all need to plan and readjust when things don't go as we expect, and never, never, never, never, never give up!

## Step 3 - Victory

VICTORY is so sweet! When you finally hit your goal, celebrate with those who helped you along the way. Buy that car if that was the goal. You will find out it wasn't really about the car, but about becoming the person you need to be to deserve that car. Play and start Dreaming again.

When you stop working the six steps of the Productive Loop for too long, you can easily slip out of the Productive Loop. You may become lax and fall into a non-productive lifestyle that can destroy all that you have worked for. Look around for guidance, and learn the methods of those around you who are further down the road than you are. Ask them how they stay in the Productive Loop, and how much time they take off after reaching their goal before they are working on another one. Everyone will have a different answer, but this will allow you to gather data and decide what is best for you.

Victory will be so sweet even for those around you. Remember, even though people may not publically be cheering for you, they are silently and desperately hoping you win your game. Everyone wants to say they are on the team when it wins, but not stick in there for the daily, monthly, and yearly practices. Be kind to everyone during your victories and take along those you care about so they can learn from you as well. Be grateful and humble, "PRIDE COMES BEFORE THE FALL!"

## Step 4 - Repeat

Make sure you continue to DREAM. All things developed in this God-Given World started with someone having a DREAM. It has always been and always will be the fuel to keep people going. A man without vision will perish. Most men die at 25 and wait to be buried until they are 75. Think about that one.

We don't feel we have arrived by any means; someone once told me I was the hardest working wealthy person they know. We don't see ourselves that way, we see ourselves as working through the journey and trying to bless as many as we can along the way. We are just little shooters who keep shooting. We pray that we will be able to keep shooting a long time.

## Principle 3 - Find Your Sign

This is the simplest principle, but in many ways, it is the most important. In order to work your plan, you need to be open to the signs that the Lord puts in your path. Right now, you may say it is coincidence, but the more you Believe, the more you will come to see that The Lord has a Plan for You. The signs are not random. They form a clear path to your destination if you know how and where to look for them.

Look for your sign. You may not get it spelled out on a billboard along an Illinois highway like I did, but you will begin to see how the pieces fit together. Enjoy your journey as Kevin and I have, and remember The Lord will guide you down the correct path as long as you are willing to travel that route. Have Faith in His Guidance.

# Epilogue

## Your Turn to be Blessed

Money is neither good nor bad; it just takes on the character of the hands that hold it. So let's all earn a lot of money and see how good we can be. I know and understand that not everyone can learn to be a consultant, but we all can learn to look for opportunities in life to help us earn extra cash. Remember, we all have to grow and develop into the people we need to be to attract people and opportunities. Mentor and be mentored. Give praise constantly, and remember it is about the team you surround yourself with. If they have a negative attitude, so will you. You will have to exert effort and have a positive attitude to grow and progress in life. If you think you can, you can. If you think you can't, you can't. Either way you are right! Don't forget to include lots of coffee and kisses along the way.

Made in USA - North Chelmsford, MA
49877_9781540464934
12.26.2023 2118